10+

THINGS I WISH I KNEW ABOUT MENTAL HEALTH IN COLLEGE

Dr. Stacia' Alexander LPC-S

Editor: Sharp Editorial

Dedication

To everyone who thought enough of the spirit beyond the earthly vessel to nurture and mold the heart of what God intended for my life.

Acknowledgments

Living on a communal plain means I need and thrive off the people around me, so I am very careful about whom I allow to share my space. My parents have loved me unconditionally and my only prayer is that they never have to experience anything beyond joy when we spend time with one another. Their commitment to my family is priceless. and I am forever grateful.

My husband, as so lovingly stated by my grandmother, is the only man who can put up with me. Our growth over the years is grounded in what God wants for our lives so that even when we are at odds, we know who keeps the fortress intact. He has watched for years as I float between home and work trying to balance my passions.

My children and nephew know that the legacy rests in them. The privilege of being a part of their lives when so many families struggle just to say hello to one another is not something I take lightly.

The many friends and colleagues whom I have bantered with about life and wellness know what it has taken to get to a place where I am at peace and in alignment. I hope they find this work worthy to share and join me on my quest to eradicate mental health stigmas.

Table Of Contents

INTRODUCTION

"You will always work because everyone needs someone to talk to about what is going on with them."
Hendu Henderson

A Brief Statement on Mental Health

The state of mental health has been percolating for the last 20 years, affecting various demographics across the spectrum of the human experience. When I started in this field in the mid-nineties, I received repeated warnings from family and friends about people not utilizing these services enough for me to maintain a reasonable career path and that I should consider another occupation.

It probably seems foolish to millions that we had to convince the masses about the importance of incorporating mental health discussions in every industry regardless of education or skill level. Stress management and employee morale were the masks to broaching the subject. Instead of talking about preventative measures to manage our lives, we operated in reactive practices that neither addressed the reasons we struggled mentally nor provided easily accessible treatment options.

Even now, society will listen to information more readily regarding therapeutic choices instead of ways to protect their psychological wellness. Many remain in denial about what it takes to have a mentally healthy lifestyle. Like our physical well-being, we must extend preventative measures for our mental health to obtain and sustain optimal cognitive and emotional functioning.

For over 20 years, I have asked clients during their intake process about their sleep patterns, nutritional habits, social networks, relationship quality, and outlook on life. And through therapy, I integrate an attempt to convey the importance of tending to one's physical body because it impacts overall well-being. I have noted when I am at my worst, and it is usually coupled with my participation in physical triggers, including high sugar intake, low water consumption, decreased physical activity, and poor sleep habits.

We are inundated with repeat messages to eat sugary and high-fat foods, drink caffeine-packed beverages, and operate on little energy to assumingly live our best lives. Communication promoting healthy lifestyle choices is constantly muted because it is associated with boredom, sleeping eight hours nightly, eating fruits and vegetables, exercising at least 30 minutes daily, and spending time with positive energy people.

The State of Mental Health for Emerging Adults

I refer to those between the ages of 17 and 25 as "emerging adults." I laugh when thinking of how I explained to my kids when they turned 18 that they were not yet "grown" until they could financially support themselves... although the government had already classified them as adults.

While working with this demographic in my private practice, I listened to them explain their frustrations with their parents intruding on their lives because they desired more autonomy. I described the process of a caterpillar emerging from its cocoon, similar to its experience at this age of life. If their parents sit back and allow outside influences to take over, it may destroy their child's chances of reaching their full potential, just like a butterfly in a cocoon with an external predator waiting. Parents stand watch, ready to protect their children, but their children need to do internal work as they prepare to spread their wings. Preparation is delicate because if the parents intrude too much, their children will not be equipped to manage adult responsibilities. As they proceed into adulthood, they continue to need guidance but with a healthy balance of prodding and protection.

Not surprisingly, people in this age group are struck with global messages to live an unhealthy lifestyle. They are on a quest for answers as they shift from their family's household into their own. Practicing a harmful régime can result in a poor diet, over-socializing to avoid feeling lonely, minimal sleep to stay abreast of activities, physical inactivity, and repeated prompts to stay on social media, which further disconnects them from healthy living.

The Mental Health of College Students

Findings from an eight-year study (between 2013 and 2021) by Lipson et al. were released in the Journal for Affective Disorders (Healthy Mind Study)[1] on the evaluation of mental health among college students using research outcomes for over 300 schools. Her team found a 50% increase in mental health problems among

1   Lipson, Sarah Ketchen, Sasha Zhou, Sara Abelson, Justin Heinze, Matthew Jirsa, Jasmine Morigney, Akilah Patterson, Meghna Singh, and Daniel Eisenberg. 2022. "Trends in College Student Mental Health and Help-Seeking by Race/Ethnicity: Findings from the National Healthy Minds Study, 2013–2021." Journal of Affective Disorders 306 (June): 138–47. https://doi.org/10.1016/j.jad.2022.03.038.

college students, and more than 60% of students experienced a mental health episode while attending college.

Take a moment to put this into perspective. If ten families send their children to college, at least six will have a mental health challenge. The most frightening aspect of this statistic is that the parents nor the students are prepared for these situations. The student may not recognize what is happening or seek help to manage the challenge. Additionally, according to the study, students of color are less likely to access treatment despite a higher rate of occurrences.

My journey with mental health during college was like riding a rollercoaster for the three and half years I attended the University of Texas at Arlington. My constant variable was learning about human behavior in my psychology classes. Reading about my symptoms and knowing there were readily available solutions allowed me to hold on to a promise I had made myself – "Just hold on and get through this, and you will be okay."

Since my time as an undergraduate student, I have helped hundreds of students identify and explore troubling thoughts and feelings. When I explained the symptoms of anxiety, one of my students asked me why anyone did not talk to her about this years ago.

Post-college graduates finding their way have also voiced appreciation for the services offered to students and wished they had access while an undergraduate. One student that checked in a year after graduation told me he knew that doing the work to heal helped him tremendously; otherwise, his life would be "messed up."

Any clinician working with college students has testimonials about gaining insight into the impact of students' mental health.

Thousands of assessments, sessions, workshops, group treatments, handouts, and crisis interventions have helped students understand the answers to their issues. More importantly, talking to professional counselors allows them to see they are not alone in their struggles.

The Impact of the Pandemic on Mental Health

The only reason I will not spend considerable time on the pandemic's effect on college-level mental health is that adequate care for the well-being of this demographic was building traction years before the COVID-19 outbreak. Before the onset of the pandemic, our mental health clinic at the college where I worked was thriving beyond capacity, requiring us to retain the services of a telehealth company to assist with the overflow. When the announcement came that the campus was closing, we immediately notified the students, explaining our services would be available in a virtual format. Unfortunately, the comfort we cultivated while the students were on campus only went so far while they lived all over the country during the quarantine.

Our students were not unlike others who grappled with isolation, low support, depression, anxiety, confusion, anger, and extreme fatigue during the lockdown. Trying to make sense of what was happening on the worldwide stage was overwhelming. Two months prior, the biggest concern was making it to class on time, remembering a work schedule, and making plans for the weekend. The fatigue that permeated during quarantine exasperated the mental challenges people already faced. Students, faculty, administration, and auxiliary staff were drained, and the most exhausting part was not knowing when the challenges would end.

The Impact of Social Media on Mental Health

A quick search of how social media impacts mental health will display hundreds of articles. The toll of access to a multitude of people "living their best lives" on social media creates waves of worry, unhappiness, and fear in people worldwide. As highly impressionable young adults, college students experience these issues more pronounced than others in society.

People are becoming more vocal and vulnerable about their mental health issues, especially with access to more information. When you see someone discussing how anxiety impacts their lives, you begin to see yourself in their storyline and realize you are not alone. If you have been suicidal, reading and hearing relatable stories of restoration can be comforting. To see others recovering from a suicide attempt and how they moved beyond those feelings is emotionally and mentally helpful.

Finally, as it relates to social media and mental health, social media can be an escape for people with human interaction challenges. Some won't go to the library or search Google Scholar to locate data on how many students suffer from depression, yet they believe the information they see on Instagram and other social media pages. We repeatedly see images of people sitting with one another and not fully connecting because social media consumes us more than in-person interactions. Isolation can be sneaky with social media because you believe you belong to a group because of common interests. The truth is, when battling life and needing human interaction, social media connections are simply not the same.

The Emotionality of Success

Speaking at colleges, I noticed students suffering from pressure to achieve. I talked to parents about the other side of high performance, stress, anxiety, and self-doubt. My goal is to help parents understand the balance needed for their children. Emotional balance is just as important as receiving high achievement awards and recognitions.

Many parents provide their children with academic assistance – tutoring, camps, scholarships, and private coaches and trainers for athletic performance. We sign them up for clubs to socialize, too. However, some parents rarely sit down and discuss their children's feelings. How are their children managing difficulties in life? Even if their challenges seem minimal, we never know how they process it all. When our children go off to college, many are not prepared to emotionally manage their new lives in the same manner as their assignments, work schedule, and social activities. Therefore, we must blend what we provide for their academic success with their needs for emotional health.

What to Expect

When I started writing this book, I thought it would be a short article highlighting notes from approximately ten years of practice. However, after a reporter interviewed me for a newsletter article, it was clear I had much more to say on the subject and needed to document my perspective in detail. And thus, this book was born.

While I attempted to be brief in each chapter, it was nearly impossible because my thoughts flowed from memories of hundreds of sessions over the years. I wish I had cataloged those instances because this project would have been more manageable. Nevertheless, some areas need more elaboration than others. So, with each chapter, I will delve deeper into issues and answers related to mental health wellness.

Parents and young adults, use this book as a guide to begin discussions; however, it cannot be used as a direct treatment option. As an aspiring or current college student, you will see yourself in these topics and learn how to notice a problem before it begins.

I wish I had this book during my tender years because the feelings of loneliness and confusion were far too frequent as I faced new dilemmas. All I was prepared for were academic studies, working to support myself, and socializing with other people. I was not ready for the cognitive and emotional challenges.

This book will walk you through other reasons you may feel discouraged, worried, and uneasy. My quest is to let you know there is help for you to manage intense feelings. At the end of this book, I offer examples of what counseling looks like for you as an adult and how to access it while in college.

Who Can Use This Book?

As a college student, you can read this book alone. Make notes about everything you need to enhance your overall mental health management before, during, and after college. Use this book as your journal. Doing so will significantly impact how you view situations and respond to them.

Parents will benefit from this book by engaging their students in open dialogue as they begin the next leg of their journey into adulthood. Far too many parents have proclaimed feeling baffled when their students display struggles with psychological well-being. Thankfully, this book provides an immediate starting point for various discussions.

The number of people who could use this book is innumerable: counselors, mental health advocates, clinicians, principals, church youth leaders, and more. Students attending college workshops generally focus on study skills, curriculum development, scholarship applications, and social skills. However, this guide will tremendously impact mental health management on campus. The plight of removing the stigma of mental health is a community effort. The more informed, the more positive strides we can make. We should all be advocates to de-stigmatize mental health in our communities.

CHAPTER ONE: GRIEF

"Too often we underestimate the power of a touch, a smile, a kind word, a listening ear, an honest compliment, or the smallest act of caring, all of which have the potential to turn a life around." - Leo F. Buscaglia

Many people associate grief with death or ending a relationship; however, grief occurs whenever an ending in life transitions you from one state of mind to another. Leaving home and going to college can bring the same emotions and experiences of loss. There is no other way to explain this disposition except to call it grief.

Going to college and staying on campus is a monumental time in life when you will experience changes you never considered because you had so much on your plate to manage. I know students focus on which classes to take, whether to take their car to school, and what it will be like to live without their parents. You will also juggle finding a roommate to get along with for an entire year, adjusting to campus food, self-managing your schedule, finding work on campus, and more.

Those are merely snippets of your new experiences in the next chapter of your life. And just like any other occasion, you may have positive and negative emotions with each step. The emotion that may take you by surprise is grief. You expect to be happy, excited, and confused as you navigate campus, yet grief is surprising. Prepare yourself for how it may look in your life so that you are not overwhelmed when it happens. Suffering is often masked by other emotions like irritation, confusion, loneliness, and anger like in these scenarios:

- Instead of acknowledging that you miss home-cooked meals, you may complain about the campus food's temperature or prices. In reality, you are thinking about your family's Sunday dinners after church.

- Instead of realizing you have a challenging time keeping up with the pace of your classes, you may feel irritated with the professor for their teaching style. In reality, you are sad and concerned that this may be too much for you.

- Instead of telling people you miss your crew back home, you fuss about the students on campus that gravitated toward each other. In reality, you feel lonely and anxious about meeting new people.

Take sharing your space with someone you never met; if you had your own room at home, this might be the first time sharing personal space with someone. You may sense a loss of privacy or space by sharing a room and bathroom. It is acceptable to miss space and privacy in college and voice that to your roommate. The intent is not to alienate your roommate. You simply miss the freedom you had at home and are adjusting to your new arrangements. Having open conversations helps to reduce irritation and miscommunication about your frustration. Pay attention to how you adapt to change and check your responses to avoid further agitating the situation. Also, remember that your roommate may have adjustment challenges, too. As you adjust to sharing your space, consider the following:

- Are you considering it a shared space, and your roommate has just as much right to comment or act on the situation?

- Have you and your roommate had a conversation about expectations regarding the shared space?

- Do you have a system for handling disagreements?

- Are you considerate and operate in a spirit of compromise?

After settling into your new space, you may feel emotional about multiple changes in your life. Being prepared for them is a huge part of meeting the challenges directly and understanding how to address those challenges. Remember, you are not alone; there are ways to get support to help you manage your life:

- Resident halls often host orientation and social events to encourage students to mingle and learn about one another. Be intentional and attend one or two, at least, to curb the edge of meeting new people.

- Speak with your advisor that helped you with enrollment and document submission. They have useful information about campus resources.

- Another coping option to adjust and garner support is talking to your parents or close friends. Make sure to talk through the situation and not just complain. When talking through an issue, you work your way to a solution. However, when you complain, you wallow in your concerns, and the issues remain after the venting, causing more frustration. So, better to focus on a solution than to endlessly vent about a problem.

Excitement

The excitement of preparing for college is multi-layered for everyone involved – students, parents, siblings, relatives, and friends. In the best circumstances, everyone prepares to equip you with books, clothes, toiletries, money, and words of encouragement to last the first semester. In the most challenging situations, you prepare to leave home and figure out life on your own. Either way, your energy goes toward the next step. Very few people look at the totality of what will change as they prepare to leave a familiar environment.

When I went to college, I moved in with a guy I was dating. I was prepared to focus on school and work. I soon realized this would be impossible while living with someone. The next semester, I moved into my own apartment, understanding it was time to stand on my own two feet. The first couple of nights alone were not necessarily frightening but unusual. Here are a few things I wish I knew before moving into my place:

- Avoid living on the first floor. There is easy access through a patio or window, which makes you vulnerable to wayward souls.

- Minimalism is the way to go. Do not spend much money on furnishings or trying to beautify your space to look like a magazine spread. Buy simple accessories and necessary items for comfort. Do not accumulate a lot of unnecessary things. Remember that you must pack and move it all at some point.

- Be frugal when shopping for groceries and essential items. You may not be able to purchase the same food brands you had at home, but you can stock up on staples (e.g., rice, soup, spaghetti), reducing your overall grocery expenses.

- Create a budget and stick to it. If you use credit cards, learn to utilize them effectively and thoughtfully. Credit can make or break you, impacting your mental health (stress, worry, and fear).

- Protect your space and treat it as your sanctuary. As you meet new people, they may want to kick back at your place, but not everyone should have access to your home. Be selective about whom you invite so you will always have a refuge to retreat, recalibrate, and recover without the negative or overwhelming energy of others.

- Clutter in your space equates to clutter in your mind. You may have grown up in a junky room, and the rest of the house was orderly. That atmosphere provided balance. Living alone in a cluttered space can leave you feeling anxious and stressed. Remove the clutter, and you will reduce the mental chaos as well.

Pre-Separation

Leading up to the big move, grief is commonly masked inside other emotions. Think about the student feeling frustrated with all of the preparations related to their relocation. There is a lot of planning for this process, and many young adults want to oversee some aspects. However, parents intervene because they understand what it takes to transition properly. Instead of addressing the uncertainty associated with this life-changing event, the student focuses on their annoyance and pushes against what is expected. This further exacerbates the parents, making the activity more complex instead of fun and exciting. When this happens, everyone should take a moment to breathe and assess their feelings. The following are questions to consider:

- How do you feel about this transition?

- Are you excited or nervous about moving on campus or into an apartment?

- What are your parents doing that you do not understand about preparing for the move?

- Which tasks do you want to do yourself (e.g., choose room decor, order campus packages, make flight or driving arrangements)?

- Are you sad, anxious, or excited as you pack and get ready to leave home?

During the Transition

During this transition phase, parents are often more sensitive than their children. They watch life shift before their eyes, fully understanding that family dynamics are about to change. Parents must come to terms with the level of independence their student requires.

While some students are busy settling into campus housing, their parents may struggle emotionally to hold it together. Occasionally, a student will notice the moment's heaviness and offer a sympathetic hug. Either of those students could be you. Sadness and grief are your body's way of processing experiences. Acknowledge the moment and commit to moving forward. Be upfront and let your family know the support you need at that time.

Finishing Drop-Off

As we finalized the details for our oldest son to move onto campus, I turned around to find him and my husband in a long embrace. They had tears in their eyes in the stillness of the room. His sister and I stopped in our tracks, his roommates paused, and everyone was quiet. It was a moment of acknowledgment, trusting our son to make good decisions, and we assured him we were only a phone call and flight away.

Dreading the impending finality of the move is usual, so there may be stalling and delay tactics to avoid the ultimate moment of goodbye. It helps to decide ahead of time how to manage the last step. Do you want to say a prayer together or have dinner in the cafeteria to mark the moment? Some parents leave the student in their dorm with their roommates and agree to talk later. Take a few moments before the big day to discuss which approach will work best for your family.

After everyone settles into their new routine, the parents head home, and the student acclimates on campus, another wave of grief may arise. Some students have a tough time waking up because they no longer hear the sounds of the household, such as their parents in the kitchen or the buzz of the garage door. Others miss the sounds of their neighborhood with sirens blaring in the distance or a nearby train chugging. A good practice is to sit for a moment to give your mind and body time to adjust to these changes. Use your senses to process your feelings.

The Separation

Every cell in your body has a memory component, consciously and subconsciously. A thought may prompt your body to miss the aroma of breakfast or how your feet feel on the warmth of your bedroom carpet. Just because you are not actively thinking about a memory does not mean your body is not processing an experience. Take time daily to adjust to your new space. The following are tips to healthily transition as you manage the direct and indirect tenets of grief:

- Use a journal to explore the differences in your daily routine, focusing on the similarities and differences from living at home.

- When talking to your parents, let them know what you miss about home to release those thoughts to someone who knows precisely what you mean and can express appreciation for your feelings.

- Be intentional about creating your schedule based on your need for productivity, peace, and purpose.

I did not miss my mama until the wee hours of the night, which was usually when I would walk to her room and check to make sure she was okay. She always fell asleep before me and was prone to seizures in the middle of the night. Every evening, I would feel her forehead for warmth, turn down the thermostat on her electric blanket, lower the television volume, and turn off her overhead light.

As I prepared my nighttime routine after moving away for college, I was keenly aware that I had no idea how she was doing, but I had to accept that reality if I were to get any sleep. On Saturday mornings, I called to see how she was doing, seeking comfort in knowing she was all right.

The Stages of Grief

The interesting thing about grief is that it is non-linear. There is no blueprint to follow and prepare for the next stage. However, there are common stages of grief, and you may experience some or all of them. The way you manage and express grief is your journey, and you need to relieve yourself of the pressure of thinking you must have it all figured out. There are people ready to retire who do not have everything figured out, so walk in the freshness of your new journey and look for positive moments to support your growth.

Denial

After you settle into your new space, the initial disbelief of finally leaving home may hit like a ton of bricks. I have students who say they were in a fog and found it hard to get their bearings when they first moved. Other students jumped right into campus life as a way to manage the denial and address the hovering feelings of sadness. The other side of denial is the difficulty of embracing the autonomy of being away from home. You may be surprised at the challenge of making every decision for yourself with little to no feedback or input from your home team.

Anger

Let us examine the levels of anger associated with grief. Frustration is a lower state of anger. You may become frustrated with the changes you are forced to endure, such as the look of your living space or your roommate's behavior. You may not like the food in the cafeteria or the times that meals are served. You may be angry at your parents for not allowing you to bring your car to school. You may experience frustrations attributed to grieving as you adjust to your new way of living. Understanding how these emotions relate to grief and the changes you are expected to balance can put everything into perspective. Learn to calm yourself by using self-regulating relaxation methods as you begin your new journey and maximize opportunities on your path. Focus on settling into your new environment and feeling grounded through these suggestions:

- Meditate in the morning and express gratitude for the areas of your life that you appreciate.

- Create a space of peace in your immediate environment with aromatherapy, peaceful or invigorating music, and calm lighting.

- Tap into artistic self-expression – painting, writing, dancing, singing, or playing music.

- Take a walk if the weather complements your energy (meaning if you cannot stand cold weather, walking on a snowy day may not regulate your mood).

Bargaining

You may arrive at school and think of a million things you left at home and could use, or you may look at items that others have and want those for yourself. Just like with the grief of losing a loved one, you may feel a sense of loss for not having the same things you had at home. To create a great space for yourself, make peace with what you have. Learn to manage with what you have instead of dwelling on what you do not have available.

Depression

While you may be among students undergoing a cycle of depression during the first few months in college, you may also be one of many that feel sad. Note: There is a difference between depression and sadness. Sadness is a milder emotion and improves over time. Depression, on the other hand, tends to be more intense, and people find it more challenging to overcome its heaviness. Depression can be situational or physiological. Situational means something happened, and your emotional response is sadness (elevating to a more intense level). Physiological means your body chemistry is made up in such a way that you have a lower or reduced supply of chemicals that elevate your mood. It may be more challenging for a person with a physiological imbalance to feel better without other treatment, like significant lifestyle changes, therapy, medication, or a combination of therapy and medication.

When feeling sad, you can attribute it to a situation such as leaving home and moving to a new area. However, depression begins to overshadow everything about your life. If you experience the following behaviors or symptoms, make an appointment with a counselor to talk through your thoughts:

- Your motivation to go through your day is harder to muster up than normal.

- Your sleep patterns shifted considerably; you sleep a lot more, or you sleep very little.

- Your appetite has changed (overeating or undereating).

- You are more irritable than usual.

- You are more sensitive than usual, finding yourself tearful or crying about things that would not have caused that reaction in the past.

- You have thoughts of harming yourself or others.

- You feel like your life will never get better.

- You find it difficult to concentrate or focus on assignments (more than your typical challenges).

- Your friends or family keep telling you that you act like something is wrong.

Acceptance

As you settle into your room, you will begin to accept changes as your new normal. When you return home for a visit, it will feel simultaneously fantastic and strange – great to be back in a familiar setting but weird because it does not fit quite as well as before you left. Some people count the days until they return home for a visit while others patiently wait for the semester break with little to no anticipation. Whatever you feel is okay.

Losing a Loved One While in College

Losing a loved one while in college may be more challenging because you are away from your family. Humans tend to grieve collectively with others who love and treasure the person that died. While your friends and teachers express heartfelt condolences for your loss, they cannot exchange the same level of grief that you share with your family and close friends. If possible, go home to be with your loved ones and spend time going through the initial grief stages with them. Inform your instructors, administrators, friends, and support system of your plans to return home. Some instructors may give extended time to complete assignments. If they do not, develop a plan to catch up on your work as soon as you return to campus.

Finally, reach out to counseling services or social services for guidance to help you manage through this phase of grief. Even if life does not seem burdensome, you may find it helpful to talk to someone to support you while you manage the loss.

If you feel heavy in your heart and mind and begin to have thoughts of harming yourself (suicide), immediately notify essential people around you (personal and professional). You may feel alone and that no one understands the depth of your pain but that does not mean you must manage those emotions alone. The powerful benefit of talking to others is that it provides another perspective to pull you out of a dark place. For students who feel like their lives will not get any better, I tell them that suicide is a permanent decision to a temporary problem.

The power of the human spirit holds on to something when feeling like issues are unmanageable. It is okay if you do not feel strong enough to do it alone. The goal is to locate the power of the human spirit, the place deep within that wants you to have a better life, and grasp onto that which is more significant. Until you do that, call on the help of others to not feel alone. People are available to walk alongside you until you feel stronger.

CHAPTER TWO: ANXIETY

"Anxiety is like a rocking chair. It gives you something to do, but it doesn't get you very far." - Jodi Picoult

The American Psychological Association defines anxiety as "an emotion characterized by feelings of tension, worried thoughts, and physical changes like increased blood pressure. Physical anxiety symptoms include fatigue, headaches, muscle tension, muscle aches, trouble swallowing, trembling or twitching, irritability, sweating, nausea, lightheadedness, hot flashes, and trouble falling or staying asleep (https://manhattanpsychologygroup.com/anxiety-in-adults/).[2] According to the American College Health Association, pre-COVID, college students were anxious at almost 30% of the student population This means three out of a group of ten have anxiety. (https://www.ncbi.nlm.nih.gov/pmc/articles/PMC8062254/).[3]

2   *"Anxiety in Adults - What to Look for & How to Treat It." n.d. Manhattan Psychology Group. Accessed October 26, 2022. https://manhattanpsychologygroup.com/anxiety-in-adults/.*

3   *Lee, Jungmin, Hyun Ju Jeong, and Sujin Kim. 2021. "Stress, Anxiety, and Depression among Undergraduate Students during the COVID-19 Pandemic and Their Use of Mental Health Services." Innovative Higher Education 46 (5). https://doi.org/10.1007/s10755-021-09552-y.*

What Does Anxiety Look Like to a First-Year College Student?

Defining anxiety for you is vital because everyone feels it differently. Think about your best days when things were going well, and life felt great. Keep that vision in mind as a barometer for measuring how you function today. How does your body feel in a new situation? Do you sweat or feel faint, nauseous, or shaky? Do you feel dizzy when someone asks you a question you cannot answer? Does your throat feel dry, or do your hands feel clammy?

Even if none of those occur, listen to your body to understand what anxiety feels like to you. Once you know its effects, incorporate ways to manage this experience, so it is not overwhelming. For some, anxiety is debilitating. There are ways to treat it to reduce or eliminate the symptoms, and finding the right method is important.

Meeting New People

The one thing about college is you will meet new people – those near your personal space, through campus activities and various affiliations, and others you see occasionally. Depending on your socialization style, this may be positive, negative, or neutral for you.

Introverts

If you prefer spending time in your own space with a smaller circle of friends whom you can trust with your energy, you are likely an introvert. Introverts typically feel more comfortable focusing on thoughts and ideas rather than what happens externally. They enjoy spending time with one or two people rather than in large groups or crowds.

Meeting new people may be challenging if you are an introvert. You will find yourself asking questions about people as you figure out whether you want to bring them close. As an introvert, you may not feel comfortable attending events on campus unless you go with a friend. Keep these things in mind as you think about doing more with others:

- Give yourself permission and grace by taking your time to decide which activities to attend.

- Think about your reason for going so you are clear about expectations and boundaries to manage through the energy of others in your physical or mental space.

- When attending events, remember your reason for attending and enjoy yourself instead of wondering what others are thinking or doing.

- Afterward, quickly review how you felt about attending the event. Think about what you liked and did not like. Examine what you would do again and what you would do differently. Do not spend much time rehashing everything. Look at it like a relay; this is just one leg of the race. Stay focused and continue moving forward.

Extroverts

Extroverts tend to enjoy sharing space with other people. They are like superheroes who gain strength from absorbing others' energy. You are an extrovert if being around others excites you rather than drains you.

Extroverts are typically gregarious and unreserved people that enjoy and seek social interaction. They appreciate meeting new people and learning about them. For those reasons, college will be refreshing and exciting for an extrovert. Be careful about overextending yourself because sharing energy with others takes from the overall reserves you may need to balance your responsibilities.

Extroverts enjoy participating in all types of activities, not just social ones. Scholarly groups, volunteering, community service, and social pursuits are interesting to extroverts. However, if you stretch yourself too far, you may find it challenging to keep up with your academic work and other obligations, which are especially important to your collegiate experience. Try the following to ensure staying on track:

- First, take care of your most important responsibilities, which will have long-term negative effects if neglected.

- Pay attention to your activity/rest cycles to ensure enough time to recuperate between activities.

- Be okay with saying no if you are doing too much.

- At the beginning of each week, gauge your effectiveness in keeping up with your assignments. Fill in other activities around priorities on your list of things to do.

Ambiverts and Omniverts

An ambivert is someone who falls in the middle of the introvert-extrovert continuum. Ambiverts have a blend of traits from both behavior styles with a knack for pulling interpersonal resources necessary to navigate and adapt to certain situations. They tend to be more flexible and neutral around other people.

An omnivert, on the other hand, embodies the traits of an introvert or extrovert as opposed to combining the two. They demonstrate behavior based on any given situation. If they are more introverted at a specific event, they do not spontaneously adjust their mood if the environment changes.

Shifting between the two types can be wearisome. So, omniverts may experience more emotional fluctuations and inconsistencies in life. For example, they can be the life of any party, flitting around the room and engaging in conversation with multiple people for hours. The following weekend, they may not desire to be around other people and feel content spending time in their own space.

Whether an ambivert or omnivert, the best tool is understanding yourself. Trying to be something you are not will put a strain on your interpersonal relationship. Be careful not to exceed your emotional limits by trying to be everything to everyone. Take time to regroup and gain balance if needed.

Managing Anxiety

Understanding how your body responds to anxiety as you manage new experiences is imperative. One thing you want to control is the impact that situations have on how you think, feel, and live. The following are ways to address anxiety:

- Journal your experiences. Journal in the evening to reflect and wrap up your day.

- Focus on how you felt and what you thought than analyzing the actual situation.

- Practice deep breathing exercises to regulate your response to an anxiety-provoking incident. It is not what happened to you as much as it is your response to the situation. You cannot control others. You can only control your behaviors which helps to manage your emotions. Use this technique to assist in relaxing —

1. Sit in a comfortable position with your feet flat on the floor, hands in your lap, palms up, and upright.

2. Close your eyes if you feel comfortable.

3. Place your right hand over your heart.

4. Breathe in through your nostrils for a count of three and out through your nose for a count of three (repeat this until you begin to relax).

5. When you can hold your breath longer, increase the count in increments of one until you reach a comfortable count.

6. Focus on breathing, feeling your heartbeat, and reducing anxiety to decompress.

7. Remember to breathe slowly as you complete each level.

- An artistic outlet can help release negative, built-up energy. Whether coloring, painting or drawing, crocheting, jewelry making, creating music, writing lyrics, or enjoying any other creative channel, those help you to reach a calm state.

- Count down from the number five to the number one, using this method to engage your senses to help your body settle down —

1. Focus on identifying five things you see (ex: bed, shoes, bookbag hanging on the back of the door, your favorite pillow, and your journal).

2. Next, find four things nearby you can touch (ex: your hair, a textbook, your computer, and your phone).

3. Then, identify three things you hear around you (ex: music, someone laughing, and a lawn mower outside your window).

4. Next, identify two things you smell (ex: cologne or perfume and a burning candle).

5. Lastly, choose one thing you can taste (ex: stale gum you chewed since lunch).

As you learn more about yourself and how you manage the world around you, think about how you respond to situations and how your response impacts your mood and choices. You have the option to respond or react. Replying to a problem means you consider variables before you respond or act. Take time to focus on positive outcomes and positive consequences for your life. A reaction is more of an impulsive act with little regard for short- or long-term effects. People who react rather than respond tend to have more negative consequences and outcomes because they do not think through their options carefully.

Anxiety is energy, just like every emotion. When you are happy, you smile or laugh. When you are mad, you frown, yell, or fuss. These behaviors expel energy from your body to express that emotion. However, anxiety is one of the emotions people tend to hold in because it is more difficult to explain. Use the outlets described above to manage your energy and see if it makes a difference in your anxiety. If the energy becomes too much to manage, seek help to learn other ways to cope to ensure anxiety does not overwhelm your life.

CHAPTER THREE: UNCERTAINTY

"There is freedom waiting for you on the breezes of the sky, and you ask, 'What if I fall?' Oh, but my darling, what if you fly?" - Erin Hanson

Where to Begin

The first time I sat in a lecture hall with hundreds of students scattered around in theater-style seating, I felt pressure so heavy in my chest that I thought someone had turned off the switch in my brain that signaled me to breathe. Nothing in life prepared me for this large room compared to the smaller classrooms I had previously visited.

I made a point of sitting in the front row of each class. I learned early on that sitting in the back gave me ammunition to watch other people instead of focusing on the instructor. The walk to the front was enough to put any person on notice; you need to watch your steps, so you won't trip. The chatter around the room absorbed the heavy sound of my feet walking down the steps, but nothing could muffle the pounding I heard from my heart. All I could think as I took a seat in the second row was whether I was in the right place and if I had the correct textbook and supplies. I watched in anticipation as the professor strolled to the podium, placed his attaché case on the floor, and walked to the board. Even though I was only two seconds from bolting, I remained calm and seated.

On the whiteboard, he wrote his full name, the class name, and the section number which all looked familiar as I checked my printed schedule. As I pulled out my yellow legal tablet from my bag to take notes, I felt the throbbing in my chest begin to slow down. I could hear students saying what I was thinking – "Am I in the right place? Is this one of the hard professors?"

Uncertainty Is Normal

Even the best high schools are challenged to prepare students for what to expect in college. Because of this, institutions fully understand that new students will need guidance during the first couple of months on campus. Most schools have orientation for incoming students and forums to speak with upper-level students about their experiences. However, your responsibility is to participate in the planned activities to help you adjust to campus life. You must prioritize those to make your life easier.

Will trying to figure out where to go on the first day of classes create angst for you? If so, reviewing the campus layout and where your classes are located before they start may be helpful.

Besides the location, the pace of college may be different from what you are accustomed to because of the scheduling patterns and length of classes. If possible, schedule your classes on days most suited to your temperament. Think about the following:

- The time of day the course is offered
- The location of the class
- The length of the class

Even though you will eventually need to take all courses in your degree curriculum, ease into your unfamiliar environment by devising a schedule to alleviate as much stress as possible.

Managing Expectations

Something else I wish I had known about college-level coursework was the expectations as a student which created significant pressure for me. I had to learn to balance my academic functions and utilize available resources to improve where needed.

While you may believe having a tutor is a weakness, a tutor is actually a primary support system on campus. Often, programs will pay for tutoring services, so it is not a financial burden on you as a student. Tutoring is an excellent study tool and reinforcement even when you believe you understand the information.

Creating a study group with people from your classes can also be beneficial. Your note-taking abilities can improve exponentially because each group partner will take notes for study sessions. As you navigate your studies, the more assertive and forward-thinking you are about your academic responsibilities, the easier it will be to go from high school to college.

Imposter Syndrome

Imposter syndrome is when you convince yourself you do not belong in a scenario or with certain people. You question your abilities although everything you did up to that point has prepared you. Unfortunately, feelings of imposter syndrome can strike at the most inopportune times, usually when you need your confidence to be at an all-time high to help you get through a situation.

You may believe everyone else has it all together, just as I did the first time I walked into a lecture hall. However, if you look and listen closely, you will discover that many, if not most people, have the same issues trying to figure out life. Some worked through this phase and feel stronger to face stressful situations while others try to make their way through to gain confidence. Conquer the same emotions of self-assurance by taking small steps:

- Remember your name! Remember who you are and that your name has previously been said to recognize your accomplishments. Your name has echoed among friends and family who think highly of you.

- Remind yourself of the hurdles you successfully jumped to get to this point.

Give yourself grace when feeling uncertain. Somewhere along the way, you convinced yourself you should have it all together, even with new ventures. That only puts more pressure on you. Instead, embrace the adventure and unknowns that come with a unique experience. Give yourself time to learn the ins and outs to fit your needs. You will find greater satisfaction in embracing the journey than fighting it the entire way by being demanding and unrelenting with yourself.

CHAPTER FOUR: SELF-DOUBT

"Don't ever make decisions based on fear. Make decisions based on hope and possibility. Make decisions based on what should happen, not what shouldn't." - Michelle Obama

You may feel the need to prove yourself. Your mind may have tricked you into thinking everyone else has it all together and you are the only one facing challenges; this is a misconception.

It would be nice if everyone wore a placard on their chest, listing their insecurities. The reason for showing this list is not to ridicule anyone but to relate with others. Becoming aware of insecurities can easily identify those with the same vulnerabilities. People tend to reach the same conclusion when mentally struggling to process their problems—they stay inside their heads. Once you begin talking to others and receiving feedback, you gather more information to make sense of your struggles. Once equipped with the appropriate tools, you figure out the best ways to work through your uncertainties. In doing so, you realize situations are more manageable than you thought. Learn to accept that you will not always get it right the first time. It is okay to make mistakes. Your response to the mistake is learned and what you will do differently the next time. Your failures are not a tombstone. Failure is a milestone, an exercise to strengthen your knowledge and resolve to be better.

Manage self-doubt by recalling your accomplishments in the face of adversity. Read affirmations to highlight your strengths. Even the strongest bridges have weak points that need reinforcement yet carry people across from one point to another. Use your strengths to carry you through dark times and work on weak areas during times of adjustment. This will help erase doubts that you do not belong.

Why Is Confidence Important as a College Student?

The simple answer is confident students tend to be more successful and have more resilience in college. The more complicated answer is a loaded one.

What does success look like for you?

What does success look like for you in the eyes of your parents? Your support system? Your community or network?

The more aligned the answers to those questions, the less stressful college experiences are for you as a student. By establishing a baseline, everyone will anticipate the same outcomes. Even if they disagree with your definition of success, they know what to expect. Unaligned expectations cause disharmony. How troublesome would it be to share with your parents that you won first place in an art contest, but their response was, "Yes, but what was your grade on that chemistry assignment you worked on last weekend?"

There are thousands of scenarios of how parents could react; however, the point is you need to be vocal about your goals for college. In turn, you need to know your parents' expectations. This may challenge you to excel or aid you in seeing the need for a discussion about your objectives, especially if they differ from what your family has voiced. The discussion is not for compliance; it's for understanding.

Resilience

Resilience is a coping construct that behavior analysts have studied for years. It measures a person's ability to recover or persevere through challenging experiences. The more confident you are, it is believed the more resilient you are. As a student, your resiliency to move through academic, social, emotional, and behavioral challenges will determine the caliber of your experiences. Achieving high-level resilience will help you bounce back from obstacles and predicaments to continue moving in the right direction. The following are ways to fortify resilience:

- Remember your original purpose for working on the task or participating in the activity.

- Embrace the positives of the journey as much as possible.

- Reflect on the lessons you learned because those often keep you from repeating errors and help you to achieve more next time.

- Permit yourself to move forward.

Whenever you accomplish a goal, your body releases small doses of dopamine into your system. Dopamine is the chemical in your brain that signals pleasure or good feelings. If you begin each day by setting goals, you set yourself up to receive small dopamine releases throughout the day, given you complete the goals. For example, by waking up a litter earlier each day before class, you then set a goal of using the extra time for prayer or meditation. By performing those simple acts, you achieve goals that enable dopamine to release organically and start your day on a positive note.

Self-confidence is vital on your college journey, and the more you develop during this phase of your life, the better you will do now and later. Self-confidence does not mean you are fearless or arrogant. It means you appreciate the skills and knowledge you acquired that prepare you for the challenges you will encounter. Build your character to help you in other areas of your life.

CHAPTER FIVE: STRESS

"Stress and worry, they solve nothing. What they do is block creativity. You are not even able to think about the solutions. Every problem has a solution." - Susan Taylor

According to mentalhealth.org, "Stress is our body's response to pressure. Different situations or life events can cause stress. It is often triggered when we experience something new, unexpected or that threatens our sense of self, or when we feel we have little control over a situation" (https://www.mentalhealth.org.uk/explore-mental-health/a-z-topics/stress#:~:text=Stress%20is%20our%20body's%20response,all%20deal%20with%20stress%20differently.)[4]

Stress is commonplace throughout campuses because the expectations of success increase astronomically when one begins college. Stress is not only associated with negative experiences. You may experience stress from joyful moments such as a first date, going to a party, or earning an excellent grade on a project. However, people manage positive stressors better than negative ones. The rush of energy from positive stressors is usually expressed freely around other people. Think about how you respond when you win

4   "Stress." n.d. Www.mentalhealth.org.uk. https://www.mentalhealth.org.uk/explore-mental-health/a-z-topics/stress#:~:text=Stress%20is%20our%20body.

a game. You may jump, scream, or emit a loud exhale. Everyone around you understands the release is coming, and they share in your joy. Or maybe someone accepted your invitation to go out, and you laugh loudly when getting off the phone. Those are times you feel comfortable releasing the pressures of the stress. However, negative stressors may be more complicated to emotionally manage. Just remember your response may be similar to millions of other college students, so you are in good company. It helps to understand and acknowledge you are not alone.

It will also be helpful to understand what happens to your body in reaction to stress. Sensations fire inside your body, sending messages to your brain, letting you know something is happening. A stressful situation may make it hard to deal with what happens around you. Some sensations you may experience are:

- Increased heart rate

- Sweaty palms

- Dry mouth

- Upset stomach/nausea

- Pressure on your bladder or bowel

- Tears

- Feeling faint

Interestingly, those sensations may cause panic because you were unprepared for them, or they cause so much discomfort that you cannot think clearly.

Keep reading.

I will provide tips to offset those sensations, so they do not overwhelm you. Over time, if you do not find a good outlet for stress, you may have physical symptoms such as:

- Unexplained aches and pains

- Stomach problems not alleviated by over-the-counter medications

- Difficulty sleeping through the night

- Excessive sleeping even though you are not exerting a lot of energy

- Migraines or other types of headaches

- Toothaches (from grinding your teeth with tension)

Stress-related emotional and behavioral expressions are as different as the people who experience them. One thing to remember – when something feels "off," it is a signal to take a closer look at what is going on in your life. Many people get into trouble because they ignore the signals and do not make the necessary adjustments. A lack of action severely impacts one's life because these issues can worsen over time. When noticing the following behaviors, your body sends warning signals to make some changes:

- Irritability

- Withdrawing from friends and others who try to help

- Sensitivity causing you to cry or fuss/fight when you generally shake things off

- Using drugs or alcohol to feel good or numb your feelings

- Changes in sexual activity

- Low concentration and focus

- Decreased motivation

Instead of ignoring stress, try one or two options to manage it. This will help to avoid burnout and the risk pits that throw you off track. A risk pit is a distraction such as relationships, drugs, social media, a bad attitude, or poor study habits that send you in a different direction from where you intended. The following are ways to manage stress:

1. Take a break. Take a step back to regroup and get back on track. Give yourself a period to decompress, rest, and plan your next steps to reach your goal.

2. Prepare, plan, and execute as much as possible to not fall behind.

3. Focus on the essentials. Be careful not to overwhelm yourself with the small things and turn them into big things. If you are not thinking clearly, seek advice or input from a close friend, campus advisor, or your parents.

4. Show yourself grace. If you did your best on the very thing causing you stress, acknowledge what you were able to do while fully understanding you may need help to do better (and that is okay).

5. Stay calm as much as possible, and check yourself. Many times, you can feel yourself losing control. Practice the relaxation techniques discussed in Chapter One to manage your stress.

6. Always take care of your basic physical needs – proper rest, sleep, and fuel (foods).

7. While a part of managing stress involves preparation, the other part is managing your response to situations. People who develop healthy coping skills tend to fare better in all walks of life, not just in college. They reap the long-term benefits of understanding how stress impacts their body rather than going through years of strain in response to stress.

CHAPTER SIX: LONELINESS

"Sometimes you need to be alone, not to be lonely but to enjoy your free time being yourself." - Anonymous

Loneliness Is Sneaky

Loneliness creeps up when you least expect it because it is an odd emotion. Loneliness happens while in a room full of people you love or with people you barely know. Loneliness occurs when you lose someone or when you gained new friends. Your response to loneliness is essential. If the feeling is short-lived, acknowledge it and move forward. However, if it lingers, talk to someone about this feeling. Feeling lonely for lengthy periods can lead to despair and hopelessness. Consider talking to a counselor about isolation and feelings of sadness. While these emotions may subside over time, receiving support lessens the moment's heaviness.

Call a Trusted Person

No one expects you to have all the answers to life just because you are in college, although this notion has been perpetuated for decades. No one knows everything right away, regardless of where you go or at what age you leave home. Give yourself permission to call home and ask questions or discuss your feelings, concerns, and ideas. Doing so can offer solutions you may not have thought of yet. Also, it helps to write questions or say them aloud. When you organize your thoughts into digestible segments, you can see things from different points of view. Keeping everything inside can lead to solutions that may not be best. Writing your thoughts helps you to look at them more closely. The same happens when talking to people you trust—you get a unique perspective.

There are different perspectives about how often students should call home to connect with their nucleus (home base or support system). You and your family need to make this decision based on what is best for you. Send cues to your parents about what feels comfortable while you are away. If you would like to be in contact with them weekly, set up a time that works for everyone's schedule. If you prefer the calls to be at random, let them know.

Another key point to effective communication is notifying your family if you will not be available for a while. For example, if you have a group project and prefer not to be interrupted, let them know so they do not worry about you. You would want the same consideration if the tables were turned.

Family is all about harmony; just because you play your piece of the musical score from an offsite studio does not mean you are not a part of the group. To maintain the flow, develop a communication style to keep the connection moving in a comfortable direction for everyone. Expect mishaps along the way because this level of independence is new for you. If your parent is more insistent about the amount of contact they desire and it becomes burdensome for you, here are a few tips to manage:

- Be upfront about what you prefer so there are no doubts or misunderstandings about the expectations.

- Be open to listening to their rationale for what they expect.

- Be open to compromise so everyone feels comfortable with the plan.

- Be open to tweaking the agreement as you adjust your patterns and needs.

Finding Your Rhythm Is Important

Your college rhythm will differ from your rhythm at home. Even in the most disorderly of households, there was a pulse to the chaos. For example, Dad may always be late for dinner even though he gets off work early. Baby brother may need an extra aggressive prompt to turn off the video game and get ready for bed. And your mom may need to open your curtains for the sun to shine through before you finally get out of bed each morning. The rhythm is the routine of the house regardless of order.

While the tempo at home was unique to your family, you must develop your own tempo in college. Discovering your pattern can be frightening and exhilarating. Many students do not schedule an early morning class because they dislike waking up too early. I was the opposite; I planned 8:00 a.m. classes because I wanted to get my studies underway. As an independent student, I also needed to choose courses to align with my work schedule.

My days consisted of classes between 8:00 a.m. and 11:00 a.m. Afterward, I took an hour nap before my first part-time job at the church daycare center, followed by my job at Liberty Mutual as a data entry clerk. I usually finished my day at about 9:00 p.m.

Spend time determining the schedule that works best for you and tweak it as needed. You always have the flexibility to change, even though your schedule automatically adjusts at the beginning of each semester. Keep in mind that you cannot change your schedule in the middle of the semester, so select your classes carefully.

Finally, if you struggle with loneliness, consider moving outside of your comfort zone. If you are an introvert and hesitate to move beyond where you are comfortable to meet new people, take small steps. Try expanding your circle in small increments to adapt as you learn about others and do more than usual.

If you are an extrovert feeling lonely, spend quiet time in prayer or meditation, whichever helps you to pause and recalibrate. This allows you the space to integrate all of the stimuli you receive and give through your contact with others. This pause will bring you to a place of peace and centeredness. It may be difficult to understand why this is important but stay with me a little longer, and it will make sense.

Think about playing a game of Jenga. When you start, all the pieces are in place, and the building is solid. As the game progresses, different players pull out a piece with the expectation that their removed piece will not topple the set. Even though the players think carefully and act considerately, they are aware that what they choose to do at that moment may cause the set to tumble. Everyone playing knows the set will fall apart, but no one knows who the culprit will be.

You are the Jenga set (the complete set). You are standing solid. Even though your foundation may be shaky, you are standing. People pulling out the blocks are your classes, your friends, the organizations you belong to, your family, you, and so forth. If you keep letting people take bits and pieces of you, you will tumble. To avoid tumbling, you must stop people and situations from pulling at you, allowing yourself time to reset and restabilize. As an extrovert, people will enjoy being around you and want "a piece" of you because they feel good around you. Pause the game to replenish yourself.

Final Statements

Relationships should have balance. During some periods, you will give more while your counterpart (romantic, friends, coworkers, team members) gives less. Then, the tables will turn where you give less, and the other person gives more. Over time, it balances so that everyone feels respected and appreciated. If you are in a relationship where you feel odd levels of imbalance, know that it is not a healthy relationship. Unhealthy relationships will often result in loneliness. Be mindful of staying in that situation too long because you may begin to think something is wrong with you instead of focusing on the poor quality of the relationship.

Another issue to pay close attention to is feeling expendable. This means you feel like the person you are in a relationship with could quickly abandon the connection without regard for your history together. Signs to watch out for are not being included in the plans and finding out later what's going on in the group. Or you always initiate contact, feel like the other person never calls you, or realize that the other person only talks about their life and never cares about what is happening with you. Those types of situations may cause you to feel lonely. Remember that energy is positive or negative. Instead of spending negative energy worrying about fitting in or being around the person treating you as if you are expendable, shift to positive energy by building relationships with other people.

You should never feel lonely. When those feelings creep up, take a step back to focus on who is around you. Instead of spending energy on pulling them back in where they are not capable of holding space for you, seek those interested in you.

CHAPTER SEVEN: FIND YOUR TRIBE

"If you want to go quickly, go alone. If you want to go far, go together." - African Proverb

Formal Organizations

Whether attending a community college, four-year university, or virtual institution, student organizations are available for your participation. These organizations are based on academic interests, social preferences, physical activities, career interests, religion/spirituality, community, media outlets, and artistic endeavors. Student groups are a way for those with similar interests to meet and develop friendships. Even though you may not have everything in common, there are enough similarities to find value in spending time with one another. Select one or two groups that pique your interest. Attend a few meetings to make an informed decision about which one(s) to join.

Socialization

Unless you travel to college with your high school friends in your luggage, you will meet new people and establish new relationships. Do not try to replace your friends from high school with college buddies. Instead, look at people through a new lens. You may learn things about yourself you would not have known had you not expanded your social circle.

Learn the Power of Discernment

Discernment is a higher-level emotional skill many people do not learn to incorporate into their backpack of people skills until well into their thirties and sometimes forties. Discernment means making decisions about a situation more profound than what you see at face value. You look at it from a short-term, extended perspective, especially when you need to make a decision. There will be people on campus from significantly diverse backgrounds. The range of people you will encounter may be challenging to figure out. Because you have not been around them for extended periods, take everything at face value. Proceed slowly and steadily as you meet new people and develop new relationships. If you feel uncomfortable around someone, do not allow pressure to lead you to continue building a relationship just because they are a fellow student or dormmate. Instead, listen to your intuition and let it guide you in determining whether you need to separate from them.

Everyone Is Not Your Best Friend

While meeting new people can be exciting, everyone you meet will not be your friend. Some people need to remain in the "associate" category. You can coexist by knowing each other's names and being cordial. It is rare to have one friend to check all categories:

- Secret bearer

- Advisor

- Travel buddy

- Shopping companion

- And whatever else you hold important for a friend

Some people fall into a few categories. Accept that you can have an exciting time traveling with someone but not trust them with your deepest secrets. You may have one friend who gives great advice but is terrible at showing up for you on special occasions. Remember your comfort zone; they have theirs as well. Asking someone to be everything for you may be too much for them to manage.

On the flip side, you do not have to be everything for someone else. Be a good friend but understand your limits. Determine what is manageable for you and be upfront about it with people as you build friendships. Give yourself time to develop solid friendships, not shallow ones just to fill time.

Leaving Friends Behind

You may find it challenging to go away to college or a new city without your high school friends. You may struggle with FOMO (fear of missing out). Interestingly, your old squad may have the same thoughts. As much as you would like to return to those "good old days," some friends have a time and place in your life. Now may be the time to move on or the time to take a break. Either way, it is time to grow.

Meditate on what awaits you when you think about spending time with old friends or going to familiar places. It is hard to leave one room and enter another simultaneously. In other words, you cannot move forward while holding on to yesteryear. This will frustrate you. To offset nostalgic feelings, plan to connect with friends over a school break. Be intentional about planning far enough ahead and doing something that everyone will enjoy.

Give It Time

The wonderful thing about college is that it opens so many doors if you invest the time to explore the world around you. You may return to your hometown during breaks and when you graduate to reconnect with high school friends. You can plan travel dates to meet up with your hometown friends or you can move on with your life and occasionally connect when time allows. Avoid putting pressure on yourself to keep everything as it was in high school. Be creative with your options and watch the world open up for you in ways you never imagined.

CHAPTER EIGHT: MEMORIES

"A man either lives life as it happens to him, meets it head-on and licks it, or he turns his back on it and starts to wither away." - *Gene Roddenberry*

Environments Matter

Just because you transferred to an unfamiliar environment does not mean all the bad experiences you had growing up will disappear. I grew up in a neighborhood where staring at someone too long was a reason to fight. I was unaware this was not the norm until I took a trip out of state. Some girls stared at my cousin and me while hanging out at the beach in Venice, California. I thought they were confrontational, but after several tense moments, I learned the girls were intrigued by the color of my volleyball. I developed a "takedown" plan in minutes while they simply wanted to play with my ball.

Later, when I thought about the "altercation," I realized the skills I used to survive in my neighborhood differed from what I would need to thrive in the next leg of my journey. Although I knew I had to stop thinking everyone was out to get me, it took several years to shed my initial warrior response to what I perceived as challenging situations.

Learning to flourish as a college student takes time. You left high school, home, and maybe the city or state you were raised in, but you now have the opportunity to make new choices. During this time of transition, many people bring their habits into their new surroundings. This can be detrimental if that style is dangerous or non-effective. For example – waking up at the last minute to get to school (some professors lock the doors to their classroom if you are late) or getting angry when something does not go your way instead of communicating with others to figure out the best solution. One more example – spending all of your money on the latest clothes instead of paying the balance on your tuition.

Simple decisions have long-term consequences at this age, and you will only dig a hole for yourself. Commit to understanding the life skills needed to be successful.

Change of Address = Change of Heart?

Just because you changed addresses does not mean you will emotionally shed responses to what happened before college. Some people experienced one or more traumatic incidents, and not everyone gets help recovering from those life-changing moments. Instead, they keep going even though they are unhealed. Moving forward without proper recovery means those feelings, responses, and triggers may arise in future situations. It is unwise to think that switching your surroundings will automatically bring healing or solve your problems. Here are some ways to notice if you struggle because of a prior experience:

- You have a short fuse with people and feel easily bothered when you believe you have been wronged.

- Your friends and family say you overreact even though you feel perfectly justified in your response.

- After an altercation, you have time to think about what happened and you regret how you responded.

- You have flashbacks of a traumatic situation, causing you to feel bad when things are going well around you.

- You avoid new situations for fear they will turn out badly.

It is particularly important to pay attention to how you feel, think, and behave. If you perceive something to be uncomfortable or unhealthy, seek help to manage your responses, so you are not overwhelmed. When you've had a challenging experience, I encourage you to include counseling in your coping resources. Utilizing additional support is one way to be the best version of yourself.

Self-Sabotage

Self-sabotage has halted many careers and collegiate journeys. You will make choices throughout your college tenure that depend heavily on what you have been taught or through observation. Were you that student in high school who achieved a lot, won many awards, or received recognition for your work, especially from your family? The feeling to perform and achieve does not disappear because you are in college. If you do not manage that well, it may cause you to put pressure on yourself in college. That pressure could result in high levels of anxiety and stress beyond what your college peers experience. Your reactions might include:

- Feeling like you need to prove yourself or outdo others

- Feelings of wanting to please yourself and others based on performance

- Looking for cheers and accolades from others when you complete a task or goal

- Fear because accomplishment can feel overwhelming

You may have difficulty processing attention and feel extra pressure. You may find it challenging to balance positive energy. So, you sabotage or short-change yourself to change the outcome of a potentially positive situation.

Another way to self-sabotage is doing just enough to get by instead of doing more to excel. For instance, you won't study for an upcoming test. By not studying, you receive a mediocre grade and tell yourself it was acceptable because you did not study anyway. You would have been disappointed if you learned and received an average grade. Instead of putting forth the effort to achieve an excellent grade, you give yourself a way out.

In another instance, you may fail to allow ample time to work on a project. Again, if you receive a poor score, you justify it by saying you recently started working on the project, knowing you had ample time to do better.

Avoid keeping score. Instead, focus on being present for the experiences. This is called intentional living.

Physiological Sabotage

Physiological compromises are also self-sabotage tactics. These make it hard for you to perform your best by putting physical barriers in place including:

- Getting less than seven to eight hours of sleep nightly

- Choosing sugary drinks instead of water

- Loading up on caffeine products to elevate energy

- Loading up on carbohydrates instead of lean proteins and vegetables

Following a simple routine will help you stay on track. If you go to bed late, sleep longer in the morning. If you love to drink soda, drink a bottle of water in between your sugary drinks. If you hate salads and leafy vegetables, drink smoothies or a protein shake. Train your body for high performance instead of conditioning it for mediocrity. Your body is a machine that will serve you long after your college years if you take care of it.

Remember the Balance Between Competitor and Cheerleader

You are your number one competitor and cheerleader. Have a balance with it all, meaning if you know you did not do your best, the competitor within needs to push for greater. If you know you did your best, the cheerleader within needs to applaud the efforts and, hopefully, the success. Balance keeps you on a forward-moving path. If you are constantly in competitor mode, you will develop self-defeating tendencies that will overwhelm you in the long run. If you stay in cheerleader mode, you will fall short of your full potential.

CHAPTER NINE: ADULTING

"Never be limited by other people's limited imaginations."
- Dr. Mae Jemison

Remember this statement – "Just because you can, doesn't mean you should."

Repeat it three times and let those words sink in.

You will encounter opportunities to participate in activities and events through your university or off-campus excursions. Some will be enticing with your newfound freedom. However, the following are questions to ask yourself:

What would my parents do?

What would Jesus do?

What would Coach do?

What should I do?

Use critical thinking skills to make wise decisions that support your short- and long-term goals. That is not to say you cannot have fun; you absolutely can have fun. However, you should not risk life or limb for the sake of drinks and laughs.

Substance Usage and Abuse

Do you remember the opening statement I told you to repeat three times? Put it into the context of substance use. Take a moment to consider the college experiences cut short because of drug and alcohol abuse. It may seem like fun to get high and forget your problems for that brief time. Unfortunately, the risks associated with toxic habits mount every time you indulge in controlled substances, including alcohol. Mediocre usage can also impact your quality of life, relationships, academic performance, and athletic functioning.

I talked with a group of students during their freshman year and was told several times that they did not see a problem with smoking weed. They made several points to justify their habit; however, when put into four categories, the conversation halted:

- Source of products

- Family and/or friends

- Finances

- Why

Drug Dealers and Product

1. Do you know where your dealer gets their product?

2. Why do you go back to this dealer? If I were a drug dealer, which I've never been, I would want to ensure my customers come back. So, I would get them to return by ensuring my crop was more potent with an extra special something. Because you trust me as your dealer, you would not question my product; therefore, I could lace it with another drug without telling you.

3. Why would you trust someone whose only priority is to make money from your usage without regard for your well-being or future?

Family and Friends

I asked those questions because several athletes and celebrities that regularly use drugs highlight their partying, seemingly without repercussions. Do you have family members or friends that frequently smoke marijuana? How do they function in life? More times than not, that person lives a lifestyle they did not desire for themselves, financially, emotionally, or in terms of quality of life. Sometimes, people with the same DNA have an addiction. If that is the case, those people have a first-hand account of what substance abuse can do to someone from their gene pool. With this knowledge, you may want to reconsider your stance on using weed, alcohol, and other mind-altering substances.

Finances

What do you spend monthly on drugs?

During my session with the students, we tallied how much the group spent, on average, on marijuana and it was calculated to be $100 weekly. One hundred dollars does not seem like a lot, right? However, if they saved this amount monthly, they would net about $4,800 annually per person.

That point hit home when I made them aware that the dealer was making $4,000 a month or nearly $48,000 annually. If the group pooled their money and invested in a property, business, or product, they could have a head start on their financial future. You should have heard the expletives when they became aware of this potential.

You can invest in a business with the money spent on substances instead of making the dealer rich. I won't say all of them stopped smoking. Heck, a couple of them dropped out of school altogether; however, after that conversation, enough of them decided to find a better way to spend their time and money, and that makes it a good day.

The Why

Outside of recreational and social use, why do college students use drugs? According to the American Addiction Center, there are several reasons students desperately search for ways to manage high-stress levels (https://americanaddictioncenters.org/blog/college-coping-mechanisms).[5] Shedding the weight of new responsibilities and pressures seems to be a critical motive for turning to substances. Instead of using drugs, try these readily available methods that do not alter your brain function and judgment:

- Walking or other activities to elevate your heart rate

- Meditation

- Prayer

- Proper sleep

- Great nutritional habits

- Hugs

- Talk therapy

---

5   *"School Stress for College Students and Unhealthy Coping Mechanisms." 2022. American Addiction Centers. July 26, 2022. https://americanaddictioncenters.org/blog/college-coping-mechanisms.*

Students with a family history of substance use or abuse are more inclined to use. Decades of research explain the elevated likelihood of repeat patterns if addiction is in the family. You can try to circumvent what is embedded in your DNA, but to what end? Why risk your overall quality of life for something that has been revealed as a potential problem in your life? Take time to reflect on the impact that substance abuse has had on your lineage and decide if you want to follow that path or change the trajectory of your heritage.

Hanging out with friends in casual settings or organized platforms (fraternities, sororities, and other social groups) is a prime way to begin experimenting with drugs. This is a word of caution and not absolute. Thousands of college students participate in organizations and never try alcohol or drugs; however, the opportunity and temptation to use are the most significant issues addressed on college campuses.

Frankly, deciding to use drugs in highly energized and reckless settings, believing you can defy the odds and not create problems for yourself, is arrogant. One thing about the typical college student between the ages of 18 and 24 is their frontal lobe (the part of the brain activated for decision-making) is not fully developed. That is why many in the 18-24 age group make reckless decisions.

What exactly does that mean?

Well, because the frontal lobe functions as the center for critical thinking and reasoning, yet it is underdeveloped at that time, youth are predisposed to taking more risks than older adults. This is why young people appear more carefree and bolder, confidently shouting YOLO (you only live once).

Circling back to using drugs in social settings, peer pressure is another crucial element and a recipe for trouble. When my son went to college, I explained that I trusted him to make wise decisions as he had in the past. But did that stop him from doing outlandish things? Absolutely not. Once, he called home from Mexico because he and his friends drove there on a whim. In another instance, we saw pictures of him on Instagram, in Argentina, petting a bobcat on the side of a mountain. We could not believe it. At that point, it was up to him to make good choices, just as it is for all college students. Even though you must live with the consequences of your decisions, think about how your choices will impact you and others who care about you.

Transparency Moment

I stopped drinking during my first year in college. Just to show you how much I was drinking, I was the person whom other students asked to run them to the liquor store because they knew I was going anyway. When I decided to stop, they were shocked.

"Lil Bit, when are you going back?"

"What do you mean you stopped drinking? Did you get pulled over or something?"

Initially, I tried explaining why I would no longer drink, but after a while, I got tired of talking about my decision. It was a decision I made, and I did not owe anyone an explanation, but there was more to it than my desire to stop. I grew up watching my mother repeat a familiar scenario every Monday – binge drinking – resulting in continuous fatigue and regrets. There were empty promises to stop drinking when I begged her to throw away the wine. As I grew, I began to ask more questions, and by the time I was in the seventh grade, I wanted answers to everything. I read about alcoholism and what it did to people because I wanted to understand what was happening to my mother. As I read, I found it surprising that alcohol was a depressant. Yes, a depressant.

While people believe they are happy and carefree when drinking, they are actually crossing the threshold of it being a relaxation aid. Alcohol is a harmful substance with the potential to do much damage.

After going to group therapy with my mother while she was in treatment, I had an epiphany. The cards were stacked against me on many levels – female, African American, divorced parents, child of an alcoholic, struggling with depression, and so on. Why would I add to this already full deck by voluntarily doing something that could be a dead end with my genetic history of alcoholism spanning at least two generations?

Something else I realized is that my thoughts of self-doubt and sadness would only get worse if I continued to drink. I indulged on the weekend while socializing, but I did it as a way to forget my problems, financial shortfalls, guys, and assignments. Even though it served its purpose, it also fed my depression. My doubts, fears, and setbacks were exacerbated when the high wore off. During group sessions, I realized that if I continued to drink, it would create havoc in my life, just as it had for my mother.

Alcohol slows down your cognitive abilities and significantly impacts your mood. The one thing I bet on was my intelligence as my path to independence. I recall looking in the mirror and saying I was a damn fool to keep drinking. I did not have a safety net if college did not work out, so I could not mess it up.

In that therapy session, I decided I had a choice, and I chose myself. I wanted to be a great person and have fun without drinking myself into an alcoholic stupor. If you use alcohol or drugs daily or recreationally, ask yourself these important questions:

- What will I choose for my life?

- How will I define my idea of fun?

- What boundaries will I set to achieve my goal?

- What risks am I willing to take?

- Have I considered the long-term impact of my usage?

Relationships

How romantic would it be to meet someone in college, start dating, get married, and live happily ever after? To my surprise, some girls majored in pre-med to marry future doctors. I was amazed at how strategic they were, quickly learning that their mothers trained them to "marry rich." They had no intention of graduating and merely sought marriage.

I was naïve, went to college, and focused on taking care of myself. I did not want to depend on anyone. Looking back, I certainly think there could have been a better balance regarding relationships; however, my primary concern was graduation.

In reality, there are many new experiences in college; dating can be wrapped up in a whirlwind of serotonin (the happy chemical in your brain), causing you to think your mate is your "everything." Yet, there is a difference between chemistry and compatibility.

Chemistry

Chemistry is a raw, authentic attraction that pulls you toward another person after exchanging energy on some level. Eye contact, enjoyable conversations, close dancing, or working together on an assignment generate chemistry. You feel drawn to a person on the purest level and feel alive when you think about them or see them.

There is no one way to develop chemistry with someone. It can be immediate or developed over time. However, it is important to act with caution to determine whether the person is authentic or has ulterior motives. You need to determine if the interactions are pure or for the sake of becoming physical.

Yes, a guy may compliment a woman or feign interest even though he has no genuine desire to date her. He plays a game of leading her to believe she is wanted and that he cares but he just wants whatever he can get from her physically. Sometimes, a woman will be deceitful once she realizes he is not someone she wants to date. Deceit crosses all demographics. It is on you to figure out if the person is really into you and interested in getting to know you.

Compatibility

Once you move beyond chemistry, consider how well you get along with someone. The rare, lasting relationships you read about relate to the couple's compatibility. Compatibility means two people get along well, their goals align, and they navigate differences well. Even though you may have setbacks, both people feel the relationship is viable and choose to continue dating.

Another critical variable in determining compatibility is how the person impacts your mood. Are you usually the best version of yourself around them, or are you at your worst because of the dynamics of your interactions? You should be around someone who brings out the best in you. If they don't, you may have chemistry but not compatibility. During the first few years of adulthood, there is more "chemistry" between college students but not much compatibility. Keep that in mind as you date.

Look at relationships as opportunities to get to know more people. Be upfront about what you like and your expectations. If you are interested in monogamous, serious dating, it is better to let the person know from the beginning. This openness will minimize confusion and hurt down the line. If you only want a physical relationship, be truthful. This acknowledgment will keep the other person from feeling betrayed. Communicating your intentions gives both parties the space to make decisions to benefit you in the relationship. Always remember you have the option to stop the relationship if you no longer enjoy being with the person. Managing this phase maturely will be better for both of you and minimize confusion.

Finding a relationship with chemistry and compatibility can be a wonderful opportunity to develop the capacity to love further. Consequently, this is good for your mental health because it releases positive chemicals in your brain that help you to have a better outlook on life. People in great relationships feel motivated and enlightened. You just need to understand the probability of meeting someone in college who will be with you for a lifetime. Enjoy relationships and the experiences you share. Dating can be an added surprise, yet worthwhile and rewarding, on your college journey.

Dating Sites

Symbolically, the world is at your fingertips, including access to people worldwide. As with social media sites, online dating requires maturity and honesty. Dating is a way to develop social skills by engaging with people outside your family and friends. Using these sites requires the same dating principles used for other encounters.

It is wise to include a layer of discretion in developing meaningful relationships, online or in person, instead of shallow encounters. Spending time with someone will add to or drain your energy. Your time is a valuable commodity, and using it frivolously without regard for your stability can cause emotional depletion and loneliness.

The last thing you want is a series of bad relationships that could be avoided if you valued your time and energy more. Learn to be satisfied with yourself and what you're doing in life instead of looking for other people to fill in gaps for you.

The End of a Relationship

If you recall, grief was discussed in the first chapter of this book. Grief, following the loss of a relationship, happens as well. While there is no right or wrong way to feel when a relationship ends, you can certainly expect grief as well as sadness, confusion, anger, or other emotions.

Take time to think about the overall quality of the relationship and how it ended. What did you learn about yourself in this process? How will you handle yourself in future relationships? Try not to focus solely on what the other person did right or wrong. Take accountability for your part in how the relationship ended, and concentrate on what you learned about yourself.

Learning from every dating experience is essential to prepare yourself for the next one. If you ignore the lessons, you are likely to repeat negative behaviors, which can leave you feeling frustrated, confused, and hurt. The last thing you want is a series of bad relationships that could be avoided had you taken inventory of what you want and deserve.

Financial Responsibility

Owing money can significantly impact your mood. Buying things at will and not worrying about paying the bill at the time of purchase may seem great, but the stress from owing money adds up. Utilize credit sparingly to avoid overwhelming yourself with future obligations. Be intentional and thoughtful about your expenditures to offset worry in advance.

While in college, minimize your standard of living, but if you spend a lot of time trying to look like you have more than you do, you will live in a false reality, which can interfere with your psyche.

Think carefully about your source of financial support in college. Will your parents send money, or will you work to earn money? You may decide to borrow money to support yourself. Make sure to talk to a trusted source, perhaps a parent or mentor, to work through the financial decisions you are forced to make at your age because those decisions could weigh you down for years if you mismanage your money.

Stages of Lifespan Development

Be careful not to overlook the primary purpose of attending an institution of higher learning – to provide a better future for yourself. Disregarding this reason is a sign of distraction that can impact your mental health and dampen your coping skills. By not developing and utilizing quality coping skills, you set the stage for more difficult experiences in life.

This development stage is like any other—you learn new skills and talents based on your acquisition of prior skills. For example, most babies learn to turn over, scoot, crawl, and walk. Each stage of development prepares them for the next.

At your age, stages of learning remain. If you cover up or ignore these steps, you will miss critical moments of development that prepare you for a better quality of life. At this stage of lifespan development, you are in or between one of two areas. Many college students fall between one or two stages, focused on figuring out who they are and where they belong and feeling productive or stuck.

People mistakenly think that once you graduate from middle and high school you know who you are and whom you want to be in life. However, you are still developing and may run into hiccups along the way. Exploration is why counselors and advisors encourage you to spend time figuring out yourself instead of spending excess energy trying to please others or fit into their ideals. Spend more energy figuring out what you enjoy, in which settings you are most productive, and what satisfies you. You will feel whole at the next juncture instead of full of regrets. Your energy is better spent figuring out yourself and what kind of life you would like to live as you move into the next stage of life.

At this point, you have the capacity to think about all relationships, not just romantic ones, and expand your concerns beyond your immediate or pressing needs. You spend time figuring out how connected you want to be to other people and how you want those connections to look. As you maneuver through this stage, you learn what makes you feel good with respect to other people and what causes you to feel lonely. The goal is to have solid and healthy relationships. As with all the areas of this book, if you have trouble having meaningful relationships, talk to your counselor to gain another perspective on managing experiences.

Struggles

Do not feel compelled to provide others with information regarding your hardships. You are walking this journey. If the weight of your responsibilities becomes too difficult to manage, remember the techniques listed in this book. And if they no longer work for you, contact the appropriate people (counselors, therapists) for help. Treat your mind and heart like a broken bone. You would not hesitate to visit a health facility to examine it. Do the same for your mind and heart. Run to the nearest resource to alleviate the pain. Be gentle and allow time to heal properly.

Unlike real life, many television programs feature college-aged adults who encounter one problem after another. The problem is solved by the end of each episode, and they all run off to the next adventure. You already know your life will not be like a television show. It may take time to work through a problem, or it may take time to recover from the consequences of a problem. Give yourself time to learn from your challenges and the consequences. Giving yourself grace in accepting your challenges is a part of creating the life you envision for yourself.

Struggles are real and may bother you quite a bit. Others may not look at their struggles as severely, and that is okay. It is up to you if you want to explain what is going on in your life. Do not feel compelled to justify your feelings or thoughts if someone does not understand.

So Much to Think About, I Know

Chapter Nine was pretty big. Its topics are subjects your parents warn you about but wish they had spent the last four years preparing you to handle. Life moves so fast even though it feels like a turtle's pace.

CHAPTER TEN: SPIRITUALITY

"It isn't until you come to a spiritual understanding of who you are - not necessarily a religious feeling, but deep down, the spirit within - that you can begin to take control." - Oprah Winfrey

My doctoral dissertation examined why young adults raised in the church do not return to their church of origin when they return from college. I cited many reasons for the shift: distractions, accessibility, or the family moving on. But one of the main variables I focused on was the dismantling of religious teachings because of human failures. I talked with people that said they are more interested in spirituality than religion. I asked several college graduates to further explain. These were their primary responses:

- They were no longer willing to feel obligated by traditions that bound them to a man and not God.

- They were more interested in connecting with the true spirit of God instead of wading through the doctrines and "noise" exhibited in their home church.

- They felt inundated with disparaging news about church leaders who go awry and very little about the thousands in alignment with God and tending to their flock.

You may want to examine where spirituality fits into your life as you make decisions about a relationship with God or a higher power. Believing in something larger than yourself is a way to feel grounded and connected. When you think about the times when you struggled or someone you know had a tough time, ask if there was a feeling connected to something greater than yourself.

When people are amid difficulties and not functioning correctly, they may feel like they are drifting and out of sync with others. This loneliness becomes overwhelming and causes folks to feel disconnected. Imagine this feeling as someone floating at sea after their boat capsized. As long as they were in the boat, regardless of the boat's size, they felt connected to something that would get them to land (a place of stability). However, when the boat capsizes, leaving them clinging to a raft or a piece of debris, they feel isolated and alone, trying to figure out how to make it to land. Even though it is the same sea, they do not feel as confident because the boat's stability is gone, similar to life and feeling connected to God or a higher power. That connection is a tether of focus, confidence, and direction.

Spirituality, at the core of its existence, is about connection. Spirituality impacts your mental health in the following ways:

- Helps you to feel connected to yourself, significant others, and a higher power as a place to begin and return when needed.

- Connecting with others creates a sense of understanding when facing challenging moments and needing support.

- Maintains connections to prevent and minimize periods of isolation and loneliness.

- Prevents or minimizes the emotions accompanying loneliness: sadness, fear, confusion, anger, self-pity, self-doubt, and more.

When Struggling and Overwhelmed, Call For Help

Spirituality is expressed in many ways. Common pathways are:

- Attending a church in the city where your college is located

- Studying spiritual writings to learn more about yourself than what you have been told to believe

- Joining a group on campus with spiritual growth

- Watching your home church's service virtually if you still have an affinity for their teachings

- Scheduling a meeting with the on-campus chaplain

- Personal worship and prayer time with music and writings that minister directly to you

Changing Religious Affiliations

"Oh, so you're really starting stuff now."

That above statement is what I hear parents say when changing religious affiliations comes up in counseling. Just as with all areas of life, you decide what helps you to feel grounded and at peace. You have a say on how you would like to worship and what religion (if any) you would like to practice. Exploration and change may be challenging depending on how rooted you are in your faith and your family's commitment to that faith. Protect your peace by being mature, informed, and communicative about your journey.

- Listen to your family as you want them to listen to you.

- Be respectful as you talk to them about your thoughts and desires.

- Decide from a place of peace instead of rebellion.

The journey is yours. Be respectful to yourself and those who care about you as you discuss your spiritual decisions. Speak with people you admire, love, and trust to be patient and respectful of you. Many who find peace and direction in their spiritual journey feel the impact of their thoughts and feelings. Embrace the process and ask as many questions as needed to move through this portion of your college experience.

CHAPTER ELEVEN: ATHLETES

"We may encounter many defeats, but we must not be defeated." - Maya Angelou

College Sports

Entering college as an athlete comes with the rewards of being in the limelight, having a ready-made tribe, and having structure in your daily routine. You may also have some people invested in your progress, which can be a blessing or a curse – a blessing because they are supportive and encouraging of your experiences, and you can count on them to be there for you, or a curse because they are highly critical of your performance even though they are supportive, causing an imbalance in the energy you need to succeed.

Going to college requires a significant commitment beyond what most people understand. An athlete's workload is double, requiring them to stay on top of their studies. Another side is that doctors, administrators, and faculty are well aware that athletes have increased instances of mental health crises, more than other students who do not participate in athletic programs. According to The American College of Sports Medicine, men and women student-athletes have a higher occurrence of anxiety. Some issues causing this is missing classes because of away games, being in front of people because of gameplay, and team isolation from other activities (http://www.acsm.org/news-detail/2021/08/09/the-american-college-of-sports-medicine-statement-on-mental-health-challenges-for-athletes#:~:text=Approximately%2030%25%20of%20women%20and,from%20a%20mental%20health%20professional).[6] Knowing these circumstances can prepare you for the onset of anxiety or depression. Things that could help include:

- Making more effort to connect with non-athlete students with whom you share similar interests to create balance in your college experience

- Staying on top of your assignments, so you do not fall behind when you are away in a competition

- Practicing relaxation techniques before game time in your own space and the locker room

- Asking the coach about resources to support the mental health of team players. This could be mindfulness sessions, group therapy, individual therapy, or more.

Let's put this into perspective and examine how your vigorous schedule impacts your mood and overall mental health:

- As an athlete, you have been regularly exercising, which is a substantial benefit for balancing your mental health. People who exercise or stay active tend to have a lower occurrence of mental health crises.

---

6   "News Detail." n.d. ACSM_CMS. Accessed October 26, 2022. http://www.acsm.org/news-detail/2021/08/09/the-american-college-of-sports-medicine-statement-on-mental-health-challenges-for-athletes#:~:text=Approximately%2030%25%20of%20women%20and.

- As an athlete, you have more amenities such as travel, festivities related to gameplay, and more direct supervision (from coaching staff), which contribute to feelings of happiness, satisfaction, and belonging.

- You can access restoration services such as those provided by the trainer when you are injured or physically overtaxed. Muscle stimulation aids in blood flow. In turn, this promotes clarity and emotional regulation because you are physiologically releasing the stress from your body.

- If you are on a winning team, you have the ultimate exhilaration of tackling goals and experiencing highlights which also helps with mood regulation.

What About When You Stop Playing Sports?

Suppose the unfortunate happens and you cannot play sports at the same level. In that case, seek a counselor as a part of your recovery team to help you manage the emotional setbacks of recovery. Recovering from any serious illness emotionally impacts some people. As an athlete, you may have the associated expectations of sadness, confusion, anger, and anxiety coupled with elevated fears of failure, low self-esteem, and tension with the recovery process. Whether you stop playing organized sports in school or post-graduation, pay attention to the mental changes that may occur after you stop playing.

- You will need to exercise independently, requiring self-motivation and discipline. Where you had external motivators for regularly scheduled activities, you will now need internal catalysts. You need to continue physical activity because pausing or halting regular exercise may have the same outcomes as those who stop other coping methods. For example, smokers who abruptly quit are often irritable and gain weight. An alcoholic can actually die from withdrawal symptoms if not appropriately treated. Be mindful of how changing activity patterns impact your mood and thoughts.

- You may gain weight or lose muscle strength if you stop engaging in routine physical activity. Many athletes have a robust appetite and routinely eat because they burn many calories daily. Interestingly, even though a non-active athlete's activity output has changed, their eating routine does not. More calories in and fewer calories out will cause weight gain. Carrying more weight can change how you feel about yourself.

- You will spend less time with team members with whom you previously shared significant hours before your injury. Even if you voluntarily leave the team, you may miss your interactions and relationships. However, if you leave because of unfavorable experiences, you may experience grief, anger, sadness, frustration, confusion, and regret. If this happens, do not ignore those natural responses to change. Understanding this possibility will give you a new perspective and not take you by surprise. Instead, you will understand what is happening. Do not hesitate to seek help to navigate this experience.

Previously, I counseled a college athlete who stopped playing sports because he was no longer interested in playing professionally after graduation. Subsequently, he stopped playing during his sophomore year and decided to focus on academics. He scheduled an appointment with me after his father became angry with him for failing some assigned coursework.

While we did not immediately find the underlying cause of this conflict, once we arrived at the place of loss related to his decision to end his athletic career, he gained more insight into how this impacted his life. Playing was not just a sport for him. It was something he did since middle school. He knew he could play on a local team after resigning from his college team but had not initiated this option because he was focused on improving his grades and graduating with honors.

Once we began talking about supplementing his independent activities to offset what he enjoyed as a player, he saw how those changes would impact his mentality. After several months of counseling, his mood improved, and his anxiety significantly decreased. While he did not stay in counseling the entire time in college, the months we met helped him gain insight into the level of intentionality needed to live a balanced life.

Balance

When it comes to your mental health, maintaining balance is about stability. Your responsibility is to maintain a healthy balance, which can be challenging.

I applaud the world-class athletes who competed at the international level in 2020 and 2021 while taking a stand to protect their mental health. They moved beyond the expectation of onlookers, organizers, and sponsors to disclose their emotional struggles. And while we should not need to know the depths of their issues, it was helpful for many people watching to understand these athletes were not exempt from mental health challenges. And for the critics, naysayers, and disrespectful people who shunned them for taking a step back, I hope they see that more people benefitted from the vulnerability and transparency of those courageous souls than from their athleticism.

Society is so focused on entertainment and has been conditioned for decades to believe "the show must go on." We ignore the rising number of people committing suicide, suffering from addiction, and being burdened by mental illness in the sports industry. Advocate for yourself by integrating preventative and sustainable habits into your regimen as an athlete. Incorporating some or all of these into your training routine, as well as during your off-season, can be beneficial:

- Spend intentional time alone each day to shed the weight of your responsibilities and reconnect with your source (faith and grounding).

- Talk to people who care nothing about your athletic performance and enjoy being around you to maintain balance in your life.

- Plan your schedule and have an accountability partner who understands the importance of sticking to it to support your goals.

- Avoid "yes" people who hesitate to tell you when you need to settle down and focus on essentials because they want something from you in the long run.

- Fuel your body correctly with nutritious food sources and hydration daily.

- Get adequate sleep, allowing plenty of time to recover physically.

- Utilize the creative arts to engage other skills and senses.

The number of benefits from playing college sports spans many areas from mental and physical health to character building, financial gains, socialization, and more. Thousands of college athletes spend hours practicing and playing sports with little awareness of how it impacts them emotionally. Be intentional about checking your mental health to create a sense of balance whether you continue into professional sports after college or stop playing in college.

CHAPTER TWELVE: HIGH-PERFORMING SCHOLARS

"Success isn't always about greatness. It's about consistency. Consistent hard work leads to success. Greatness will come." - Dwayne Johnson

Those who reach phenomenal levels of academic accomplishments in college may also experience challenges with mental health that they are not prepared to address.

Some years ago, I spoke with a group of parents preparing their senior students to graduate high school and enter college. These students attended a college prep program, so everyone was certain their child would continue to higher ed. When I started talking about the levels of stress their children process daily, a mother in the back of the room yelled out, "Speak!" as if we were in the middle of a church service.

I facilitated a group discussion to help them understand that accomplishments and high achievements do not mean their children are immune from mental health challenges. Regardless of academic prowess and IQ, the development cycle remains the same across the board. Even though a student may be smart enough to skip to a higher grade and attend college at 15 years old does not mean they are socially and emotionally maturing at the same rate. The issues of self-doubt, wanting to belong, feeling overwhelmed, and other emotions continue to occur despite academic achievements.

Interestingly, as a high-achieving scholar, you may feel more compelled to hide your difficulties because everyone expects you to have it all together, just as you do with your academics. Regardless of how well you outperform other students, you may fare better with a supportive community to help you maintain balance in all areas of your life.

We absorb and share energy with those around us. Far too often, I see students severely limit their time with friends and family because they study more than the typical student. If you try to function outside of that circle of energy, you make it harder for yourself to maintain the balance needed for overall success. Even if no one understands you, let someone know when you're having a tough time. You have options as a student:

- Talk to a counselor.

- Get a mentor to offer direction on navigating the coursework and projects you are managing.

- Work in a group setting.

- Use a journal to record your thoughts and feelings.

- Integrate mental health breaks into your busy calendar to make sure you are just as important as your next assignment or project.

Success and accolades do not make you immune to emotional challenges and shortfalls. Success and accolades may make you more susceptible because you pay more attention to your academics and accomplishments, not fully realizing you are slowly becoming more overwhelmed. By maintaining a solid connection with others who genuinely support you, you create a haven to maintain balance. Your IQ does not erase your need for emotional connection.

CHAPTER THIRTEEN: COUNSELING

"Thoughts disentangle themselves when they pass through the lips and fingertips." - Dawson Trotman

Let's begin with a few key points to remember about counseling:

- Counseling is more than a crisis tool.

- You have the final decision regarding who and what specialty of counselor to manage your mental health.

- What you discuss in counseling is private (with certain conditions).

- There is no timeline on how long or often to attend counseling.

Counseling is more than a way to manage your mental health and intense moments in life. You can use it for lifestyle management and stress prevention. After a few sessions, you may see how counseling impacts your ability to understand your emotional behavior.

One of the biggest hurdles to overcome in the advocacy for mental health wellness is the stigma associated with participating in regular counseling services. For so long, many believed counseling meant you experienced a mental collapse, placing you at risk and not allowing you to live a "normal" life. Had we shed the century-old stigma, we would not have the depth of emotional affliction we experience in society today. People were so intent on denying or ignoring the emotional response to hardship, challenges, and shortcomings that they failed to see how the generational growth of dysfunction impaired entire households and communities.

A Lifestyle Management Tool

Think about resources you use periodically to enhance your quality of life. You visit your physician annually for preventative medical care and your dentist biannually to tend to your dental needs. Perhaps you work with a tutor as you prepare for midterm exams to ensure you understand the concepts. You may have a trainer to enhance your athletic performance. Going to counseling as a lifestyle management tool is in the same vein as those maintenance resources.

"But I can talk to my mom (or dad) if I have a problem."

"My pastor told me I can call him any time I need to talk."

"My friends will hold me down if I run into a problem."

I have heard those statements more from students when talking about integrating counseling into their wellness routine. The important thing is all of those statements are true, especially when you need the perspective of someone you trust. However, integrating a professional counselor into the equation offers an extension of support that gives you the space to work through your experiences without bias. Additionally, those close to you may feel challenged to see patterns of behavior that need attention or call you out on your stuff.

Counseling as a lifestyle management tool should be incorporated into each phase of your journey, so it does not feel foreign to work through experiences with a counselor. Find someone with whom you feel aligned, with the same values, and with whom you feel comfortable talking about your life.

Finally, clinicians study human behavior with the anticipation of helping you resolve distress and guiding you in developing life skills to avoid making choices that throw you off track. Repeatedly going to confidants with your problems impacts the bond. I have talked to many people who realized they unloaded their issues onto family or friends too often, putting a strain on the relationship, which is highly unlikely to happen with a professional counselor. Protect the energy of your friendships by managing the time spent talking through your problems.

How to Choose a Clinician

Until this point in your life, your parent or guardian chose just about every professional for your life and health. Take the time to look at the traits or skills of counselors as you decide which is best for you. Counselors are not the same and do not have the same specialties. Your choice relies on your goals and what is happening in your life. You may work with one counselor for a while and later decide that you need another type of counselor specializing in that area. For instance, first-year college students may use counseling to boost their coping and life skills to manage the pressures of college. However, by senior year, they may want to work through childhood trauma and need a counselor specializing in trauma recovery.

I often tell people they are under no obligation to stick with a counselor forever. You have the privilege and option to decide based on the answers to the following questions:

- What are your goals for counseling, and have they changed throughout the course of therapy?

- How are you progressing in therapy with your counselor? Is your counselor aligned with your goals and what you hope to achieve?

- Are the counselor's methods effective for your needs? Do you see growth after a period of working with them?

Not surprisingly, people tend to feel more comfortable with people they believe understand their background and life experiences. Therefore, it is best to be honest with yourself about whom you prefer to work with, as it is a very personal choice.

Counselor/Therapist/Psychotherapist/ Social Worker

The field is multi-layered, and very few people understand the initials behind the names of thousands of professionals. All licensed clinicians must have an undergraduate degree, which could be in one of a hundred or more areas of study, except a chemical dependency counselor. The graduate and doctorate levels are where you begin to see the clinician's choices for their specialization.

MA and MS: Master of Arts and Master of Science (counseling, psychology, social work, marriage and family therapy, and several more). They are required to obtain licensure in their state to practice as a counselor.

LMFT: Licensed Marriage and Family Therapist

NCC: National Certified Counselor

LCDC: Licensed Chemical Dependency Counselor

LPC: Licensed Professional Counselor

LMHC: Licensed Mental Health Counselor

LCSW: Licensed Clinical Social Worker

LMSW: Licensed Master Social Worker

Psychologists

Ph.D., Psy.D., Ed.D.: Doctorate with a focus in counseling, psychology, social work, or education. They go to school beyond the master's level and further their field of study. They conduct more research to fully understand therapeutic concepts and techniques. In most cases, they cannot prescribe medication.

Psychiatrists

MD and DO: Clinicians who completed training in medical school and focused on behavioral health. They do not provide traditional counseling services (although some do) but conduct an extensive intake process to determine your issues and treatment needs. They prescribe medication should the two of you deem it necessary to manage your mood, behavior, and disorders.

What Does Counseling Look Like as an Adult?

After choosing a clinician to suit your needs, arrange the first appointment. You must call their office or complete an online form to begin the process. Remember, this is not the actual appointment, so you will not need to go into great detail about your reason for counseling. You will do that at the time of the intake appointment. Before you call, make sure you are prepared to answer these questions:

- What is your reason for seeking counseling services?

- Are you in the middle of a crisis?

- Do you feel like you will harm yourself?

- Would you prefer virtual or in-office counseling?

- What day and time work best for your appointments?

- Will you use insurance or pay out of pocket?

After you make an appointment, record it on your schedule. Put a reminder on your phone a few days prior so you will not forget. If you need to complete paperwork, arrive approximately 15 minutes early for your appointment. Prepare to remain in the office or session for at least 45 minutes, although some counselors have 50- or 60-minute appointments.

Be open and transparent during your session. The counselor is not a mind reader or a magician, so they rely on your disclosure to learn more about you and the best way to guide you on your journey. You will learn if you want to keep seeing them as your counselor.

After the first session, consider your counselor to ensure they fit your needs. Depending on your reason for going to counseling, the session may have rough moments for you. Several emotions are felt following a session; you may feel optimistic since you could talk about issues to gain clarity and direction for your life or despondent because everything is still a mess. Or you may experience sadness, confusion, anger, or a myriad of other emotions.

Be patient with the process. Keep in mind this is your real life, not a TikTok-edited post or a pre-recorded reality show where everything resolves in a matter of minutes. It may take time to see change or improvement. The primary focus is your openness to receiving help and finding the right counselor for you. As an adult, you are responsible for managing your appointments.

- Arrive on time.

- If you must reschedule, do so at least 24 hours in advance. Avoid missing appointments without notifying your clinician. You will likely incur a cancellation fee if you do not cancel in advance.

- Respect the time assigned for your counseling appointment.

- If you are in a virtual session, ensure your privacy by settling into a quiet, secluded area, much as you would at the counseling office.

- Reduce disruptions by silencing your phone during the session.

- Use a journal during the session to remember key points to reflect on later.

Costs

There are multiple ways to pay for counseling, and it may require research if your student fees do not cover the service. You will need to call or visit the counseling center and follow their intake procedures if services are included. If your campus does not have a counseling office, speak with your advisor about community partnerships that provide counseling services. They may have a resource list of providers who offer no cost or reduced fees for treatment.

Another option is to call your insurance program to see what benefits are available under behavioral health care. You may have a co-pay per visit, but they will explain this to you. There is a chance your plan has a deductible, meaning you will pay the entire cost until you reach a specified amount. You may need to speak with your parents regarding the insurance package. If so, get the details of the plan and coverage for counseling.

Some people have access to an EAP (Employee Assistance Program) that covers a specified number of sessions annually at no out-of-pocket expense for the user. Speak with your parents or the insurance provider for specifics. Expect a limited number of clinician referrals based on your EAP and limited sessions (generally no more than six in 12 months without special approval).

There may be non-profit organizations that pay for counseling services for those within their immediate community. It is worth scheduling time with your parents to review your behavioral health care options before school starts, so you do not try to search during a crisis.

Therapy is a collaboration between you and your therapist. Expect to be involved in the process. You are the expert in your life, and the therapist is a guide. Prepare yourself to take ownership of your actions and work on strengthening areas of your life causing distress.

CHAPTER FOURTEEN: AFTER COLLEGE

"Your work is going to fill a large part of your life, and the only way to be truly satisfied is to do what you believe is great work. And the only way to do great work is to love what you do. If you haven't found it yet, keep looking. Don't settle. As with all matters of the heart, you'll know when you find it." - Steve Jobs

I am almost sure no one has talked to you about what to expect psychologically and emotionally following your time in college. Everyone focuses on graduating, finding a job, and finding a place to live. People minimize or ignore the mental health needs of students once they complete their studies.

After finishing three levels of higher education, it was not until I completed my doctorate that I realized I had symptoms of post-traumatic stress disorder (PTSD). I only used three and a half years to complete my first degree and sailed into my master's program the following semester. After finishing my counseling degree, I took time off to manage my family life. When my youngest child started kindergarten, I entered my doctoral program. It took me 12 years to complete my last degree in clinical psychology, the same year my youngest completed high school.

You can imagine the summer whirlwind of going through graduation festivities and preparing for her first year in college. I was so caught up in what she needed that I had little time to think about my impressive achievement. It began to sink in about six months later when I realized how difficult it was for me to relax on the weekends and evenings. In the back of my mind was a paper to read, an assignment to complete, or a discussion question to answer. I had a feeling of doom that I had forgotten something. I had to keep reminding myself there were no assignments pending so I could relax. Heightened levels of anxiety are commonplace for people after they finish college.

Recent graduates tell me about their struggles when they no longer have the routine of class or papers due. Without that familiar structure, they found it hard to complete the most mundane tasks because no one was waiting on them to submit proof of completion.

I have heard graduates from all levels of education say they suffered more now from fear of failure than before graduating. They felt increased anxiety about succeeding in life. The tangible presence of the college degree added pressure to their lives.

Another experience with new alums would be the loss of their social circle, especially if they moved to another town. Just as they experienced grief coming into college, they experience it at the end, too. While in college, you build a "family," and starting over may trigger the same emotions you had when entering college. Acknowledge those feelings and give yourself time to adjust. The grief this time around may not have as big of an impact because you have learned new skills in college and how to manage those emotions.

The students who leave college without graduating have similar experiences post-college. They also process thoughts of failure, occasionally arising from not completing an endeavor.

Early Withdrawal

One moment did not define your life when you decided to withdraw early from college. Maybe you had to stop attending due to finances, poor performance, stress, or a change in interests. The next step will be to hold yourself accountable for whatever part you played in the need to exit your program. In every experience, there is always a lesson, whether joyful or painful. Figure out what lessons lie in the experience and how they can help you to become a better you.

Lessons are the fountain of wisdom. It is not about growing old but learning from experiences. Do not let your experience be fruitless. Lessons give you tools to manage your life and gain peace. If you ignore or minimize the lesson, you will likely repeat the behaviors that caused your problems, pushing you further from the harmonious life you desire.

Set your short- and long-term goals. Be precise. Short-term goals are what you envision and need to accomplish within the next six to 12 months. Your long-term goals are at least one year away and can extend as far as you want. Prioritize goals based on the level of importance and impact on your life. For each goal, establish an action plan with as many details as possible for your steps. Your plan of action needs to include:

- The steps you need to take to accomplish the goal

- The support and resources you need to achieve the task

- The timeline you need to complete each task

- A list of milestones or barriers and how you plan to address them

- A statement of what it will mean to you and your life when you accomplish the goal

Leaving college, whether through graduation, transfer, or early withdrawal, has an emotional response, so pay attention to your response. Do yourself a favor by looking at your response to the experience instead of jumping into the next thing without fully understanding the impact. If you are the type of person that quickly recovers and moves forward, okay. If you need more time to adjust, okay. Pay attention to the emotional and cognitive signals your body sends you and respond accordingly regarding how fast the world is moving around you.

CHAPTER FIFTEEN: RESOURCES

On-Campus Counseling

With the expansion of mental health services, many colleges incorporate treatment options into their general healthcare and student services. Just as you investigate the recreational facilities, residential housing options, student groups, tutoring services, and meal plans before attending your university, incorporate a tour of the healthcare programming to see if it includes options for mental health treatment. Some college counseling centers are robust with well-established programs. Other campuses have smaller counseling centers and may offer one or two options for students. The range of services can include:

- Individual counseling
- Couples counseling
- Crisis management
- Conflict resolution
- Group treatment
- Suicide crisis help
- Multiple counseling platforms (in the office, virtual, telephonically)

While there may be a cost associated with receiving on-campus counseling services, it should be minimal or covered through your tuition (via student service fees).

On-Campus Social Services

If you require assistance beyond the counseling office, some schools offer programming related to housing assistance, clothing, meals, and situations not addressed directly through academic studies.

The reality is not everyone has a family or support system to help them while in school. If you need help not offered on campus, talk to your advisor or admissions counselor about community resources. Associating with a local church or organization near your campus may offer options. Some churches consider it their privilege to help college students in their area and may have a support program to assist you.

Virtual Counseling

As with the transition from in-person learning to a virtual format, there has been a shift in counseling services. Ask about the options available to you as a student. It may also depend on the type of counseling you need and whether virtual sessions are available. For instance, virtual counseling may be available for crises and transferred to in-person treatment for ongoing services.

Parental Support

Ask your parents to provide access to a credit or debit card to use only for scheduling a counseling appointment. Have a mature conversation with your parents about using it specifically for this purpose. I used this option for our adult kids and suggest it to others who can do so, too. In turn, you are old enough to be responsible and use this benefit only for accessing counseling services or other mental health services. Do not manipulate the privilege by misusing it to buy an emotional support animal, adult coloring books, or other items you deem necessary. Talk to your parents before purchasing other aids to help with your emotional and cognitive management. Access to this support method allows you to maintain autonomy when seeking mental health assistance without explaining when you schedule an appointment.

Non-Profit or National Organizations

- Call 9-8-8 for mental health emergencies
- Call 9-1-1 if there is a physical emergency
- STEVE FUND Crisis Text Line: Text "STEVE" to 741741 (hotline for students of color)
- Jed Foundation: Text "START" to 741741 or call 1-800-273-TALK (8255). www.jedfoundation.org
- National Suicide Prevention Lifeline: 1-800-273-8255
- National Suicide Hotline: 1-800-273-TALK (8255)
- American Foundation for Suicide Prevention: https://afsp.org/
- Active Minds: www.activeminds.org/
- SAMHSA: www.samhsa.gov/
- NAMI: www.nami.org/
- Mental Health America: www.mentalhealthamerica.net/
- Mental Health First Aid: www.mentalhealthfirstaid.org/cs/

CONCLUSION

As I wrote this book, I realized a wealth of information was included, but all of it is necessary because students have frequent mental health challenges. I also wondered if students would read the entire content because it covers many topics. Nonetheless, I followed my heart, knowing that if I had this book before entering college, many things would have made better sense to me. I searched for answers in my psychology and philosophy classes and electives courses. I read books during every break to learn more about myself because I thought no one could provide answers to my experiences.

My first encounter with counseling was right out of high school at the urging of a guy I dated. The counselor was so confrontational that I vowed to do the exact opposite of her approach when I began to counsel people. Even with that experience, I never sought counseling when I went to college. There were no signs those services were available, nor did I connect with a professor I trusted to confide in about what was troubling me when I became overwhelmed.

I hope that high school teachers and counselors will incorporate this book into their college readiness programming just as heavily as workshops on building study skills and choosing the best college. This book is beneficial for colleges worldwide to provide in their orientation cycle and offers a way to guide students through its information. If students take psychology courses, they can utilize them to help future mental health providers understand the importance of working thoroughly with this demographic at such a crucial time in their lives.

On one of my social media pages, I recently shared about traumas that followed me into college after I thought I left them behind in high school. A follower shared her support for my thoughts because her son committed suicide in college. I am certain my parents were unaware of my struggles until I called my daddy weeping one night. I was crying so hard he could not understand what I was saying. Through the pain in his voice, I heard him apologize for not being there and being unaware of my battle with anxiety, depression, and other fears. In trying to give me space while I was away at school, we did not talk as much. This changed with that phone call. Since then, we have not gone more than two weeks without talking to one another.

How many parents do the same, not realizing their adult children are having a tough time? In trying to give them their independence, parents miss the silent cues that their child struggles with at this stage of life. Hence, the next group of people I envision using this book is parents, along with their emerging adults. It would be so powerful for households to use this book during high school (junior and senior years) to prompt the hard but necessary conversations many are afraid to broach.

Each chapter is a place to start a conversation with help on how to navigate the outcomes. One benefit of discussing the content is demonstrating to young adults that their parents are interested in more than grades and their chosen profession. It will reflect a desire to genuinely understand how the student copes with their current path. It will also help determine the level of support needed along the journey.

For parents, this book provides a baseline to understand where their children are in terms of mental health needs. This information can prevent feeling paralyzed and inept when their kids face difficulties. By having in-depth conversations, this book may remove insensitivity to what their kids experience. Moving beyond shallow and general, "how are you doing" questions to a more profound "how are you doing?"

And, naturally, clinicians in private practice are the last group that will find this book helpful. An astronomical number of college students do not access campus counseling and clinical resources. While this book can be used as a guide in private clinical settings, it should also be on their referral list of resources for student and parent usage.

www.ingramcontent.com/pod-product-compliance
Lightning Source LLC
Chambersburg PA
CBHW041225280326
41928CB00045B/64